# CO-PARENTII
# WITH A NARCISS...
# EX

How to Protect Your Child
from a Toxic Parent & Start Healing
from Emotional Abuse in Your Relationship
Tips & Tricks For Co-Parenting With A Narcissist

# Contents

# INTRODUCTION

I f you have a narcissistic partner in your life, you know the pain this can bring. Not only are you dealing with an emotionally deficient individual who refuses to acknowledge their shortcomings or apologize for past mistakes, but now you're co-parenting with one of these persons and putting trust back into the relationship. You may be wondering how someone is supposed to do this in the world, especially when their ex has never been trustworthy throughout their entire life. The best way is to have a calm and rational discussion about the future.

You're in no position to dictate what your children should or shouldn't do, but you can determine whether or not you want to be around your ex, and you can decide which parent they should spend time with.

If you're the narcissistic father or mother, you need to think about your role in this seriously. You'll need to sit down with your ex and discuss how you would proceed with the children. You don't have to be in love or anything close to it, but you do have to collaborate on whatever plan is agreed upon for the benefit of the children.

The process of co-parenting with a narcissistic ex can be challenging. It's hard for both parents to rebuild trust; it's easy for the children to question your motivations; and the situation is costly, not only from lack of money going into a giant pot but also from all the therapy that needs to be done.

Yet, despite the time and energy it takes, it's still worth doing.

For starters, even if one parent is more than happy to be done with the other, they have a responsibility to act in the children's best interest and, therefore, must co-parent in some capacity. It's also essential for the children's emotional well-being to get to know both parents and not grow up feeling like one of you doesn't exist.

And let's face it, their well-being is intrinsically linked to yours. They will always be in your life, and you want to make sure they're healthy and happy adults.

So even if you hate your ex and are happier without them, have an adult conversation with yourself and determine how many hours a week you're going to spend communicating with or thinking about your ex outside of scheduled time with the kids. And then do it. It will not be easy to do, but it will be well worth your time.

With that commitment, you can focus on your recovery and co-parenting with a narcissist instead of being consumed by anger and resentment.

The hardest part of co-parenting is putting trust back into the relationship. If both parents do not entirely agree about the course of action, they will have to communicate and talk through decisions that affect them both.

If one or both of you still believe the problem is the mother, you'll never be able to work together. If you don't believe in your ex's ability to parent, you will never feel truly comfortable with them as a co-parent.

You'll always be worried that your ex will make a mistake and take it out on the children, but if you're willing to put those fears aside and let go of the past, then you have a chance to rebuild and trust.

**It's not always a smooth ride, but it is possible.**

# PROFILE OF THE NARCISSIST

Narcissism is a character trait in which someone displays heightened overconfidence due to their admiration; they can do no wrong. This is an exaggerated behavior that breathes and exudes arrogance, pretentiousness, and a deep-rooted ideology of false superiority. "I am special. Everyone else in the world is below me because they are not me."

A person who exhibits narcissistic characteristics is often described as cocky, self-centered, self-absorbed, and rude. They view life as a playground for manipulating emotion, as an untapped market to exploit and bend the truth at will. They can be viewed as "winners," but they are crude people to be involved with due to their self-described perfection. So, too, are they, liars.

Their success — in most cases — is because of their total and complete disregard for other people and their feelings. Or rather, narcissists will push past people no matter what those people are feeling. They view other people as obstacles. We are their next hurdle to get over. They would most likely push us off the edge of a top-floor balcony if it meant that they would get just a little more ahead of everyone else.

Narcissists are the perennial interrupters of conversation. They constantly crave the limelight; they feel they deserve everyone's attention at every single turn. They want to be seen. They want to be heard. They want to be the leading figure in any small gathering, work circles, friendship circles, and among the large crowds. They are the people who ooze confidence in every moment.

They are very charming people, and more often than not, they are quite funny, very sarcastic. They are good company in public, but once at home and in their respective comfort zones, they shed their charming skins for the emotionally deprived, ostentatious colors that they don when returned to their private and intimate places. They use manipulation and excessive, yet believable, lies as a tool to such an extent that narcissists are almost fanatical individuals regarding their use of such methods.

Narcissists have such a deep self-belief burning within them. But with all of that lies a person who has been deeply affected by life. Narcissists are people, though pretty hardcore ones, who past trauma, past experiences have shaped, or past abuse, which, in turn, has crafted them into a person with such anxiety that the line between nervousness and abandonment has morphed and blurred into a singularly, individualistic focus that the admiration that they are constantly seeking is due to their inner mental conflicts that were borne from a lonely and possibly unloved childhood.

This has made them develop what we could call external spotlighted arrogance. The definition of this is a spotlight. Some form of an inner spotlight externalizes itself – or switches on when it feels like it needs to be seen. It burns so bright that it forces people to shift and focus all undivided attention on the narcissist. If looked at from a psychological perspective, this trait or behavioral characteristic is most common in children below the age of 10. It is that need to stand out from the rest, to get attention, whether that is from your parents, family, friends; it's a phase our brains go through during early childhood development that can be best linked to the behavior of being boastful or to brag about something. In a narcissist's case, what they are essentially bragging about is themselves. We all know a narcissist. They could be our mother or our father; they could have been this way for as long as we can remember and have left us, now in adulthood, shattered, confused, exhausted. They could be our brother or our sister; they were always showered with praise, always told that they were the star. They were serial winners and developed an egotism that has become the prospective difficulties in our lives, still affecting us at this very moment. They could be a work colleague or an employee. But what are the roots of narcissism?

Narcissists tend to view themselves quite differently when compared to others, and they often make those around them feel inadequate and devalued. Here's the kicker – a narcissist always wants everything to be about themselves. You might not mind showering a one-year-old infant with all your attention, but you will start to mind when a 35-year-old demands the same level of attention and achieves it at your expense. Narcissists easily victimize others by just being themselves, and it is unlikely they will ever change. This might seem rather severe, but you will not realize how toxic such individuals can be until you deal with a narcissist.

## Where Does Narcissism Come From

Narcissism usually develops in early childhood. People say many times that narcissistic behavior reminds them of a toddler throwing a tantrum.

It seems the emotional trauma responsible for narcissism occurs around the age of a toddler. Hence the narcissist's ability to handle emotions gets stuck at that level of mental development. That explains their dangerous emotional immaturity.

We all get exposed to trauma during the early stages of our development. It's simply inevitable. Trauma results from something as simple as not being picked up by our parents as a baby or being fed against our will. It could also result from something more severe like our mother leaving us at the kindergarten for the first time, which can cause a long-lasting fear of separation. Our parents fighting and screaming at each other in our presence can leave its imprints on our subconscious mind, too. So, what kind of trauma produces a narcissist?

Growing up with an overbearing or completely neglectful parent can warp a child's mind and cause them to be narcissistic adults later in life. A parent can be overbearing when it comes to a child's performance in school and neglectful when it comes to the child's emotional needs.

The trauma of a narcissist is the perceived lack of control. The inability to acknowledge their own emotions makes a narcissist extremely uncomfortable. Admitting one "wrong" thing about themselves would make them feel as though everything is wrong. So, every abusive and manipulative action they take only serves one purpose: to feel in control. The root of their toxic behavior towards you has nothing to do with you, and it has everything to do with them. If you pay close attention to their accusations, you will see that they project their behavior, fears, and doubts on you. A narcissist may often lie yet accuse you of lying all the time, no matter how much proof you present that they are wrong. They may feel as if everyone is out to get them and always get the short end of the stick, so they project their subconscious beliefs on you by accusing you of plotting schemes against them every time there is a simple misunderstanding.

You must keep in mind that narcissists never truly learned how to express and process their emotions. Their parents may have been overly protective and proud of them—but only when they fulfilled their parents' expectations. One could try to do some research about the past of the narcissist in question. Though it usually is difficult to get a clear picture. It's very difficult to find the truth about a narcissist, especially when their parents admit to not handling their child.

In many cases, one or both of their parents may display some narcissistic traits, too. However, that does not mean that the children of a narcissist are bound to become narcissistic as well.

It's not up to you to determine why the person that treated you so badly has become who they are today, and it is also not necessary for your recovery process. However, what is necessary for your recovery process is that you are aware that it's not your fault in any way that they are a narcissist. With that, you are not responsible for their chronic toxicity. This can be an environmental cause that can lead to a forced image of perfection later in life. Another aspect is early childhood abuse. One best way to deal with abuse is to see yourself above it, too clean for it. Taking an abusive history into account, narcissism acts as a wall to prevent being hurt further in the future. Despite the several ways the disorder can be environmental, some believe that the trait can be hereditary. With genetics, though, seeing a specific behavioral trait can be difficult. Often, though it may seem genetic, it is moreover the way that parent or grandparent was raised that gives them the condition. This brings up the question of actual genetics. Science has yet to come to a clear conclusion on that, though. Studies have not been able to come to a solid decision, and with many different conditions, it is hard to see which is environmental and which is genetic.

# HOW TO UNDERSTAND AND RECOGNIZE THE LANGUAGE OF THE NARCISSIST

You can tell if the person you are in a relationship with is a narcissist based on their behavior. Ideally, you should be able to figure out if your boyfriend, girlfriend, or even an acquaintance has narcissistic tendencies as soon as possible so that you can sever ties with them before you are too invested in that relationship. Here are ten points that a narcissist will always do in a relationship.

## He Will Try to Charm You

Narcissists can be quite charismatic and charming when they want something from you. If you are in a relationship with one, he will go out of his way to make you feel special in the beginning so that you trust him enough to let your guard down. As long as you are serving the purpose, he wants you to serve. The narcissist will give you a lot of attention and make you feel like the center of his world. If someone puts you on a pedestal during the early stages of your relationship, you should pay more attention to the way they act to see if they are faking it.

## He Will Make You Feel Worthless

After hanging out with a narcissist for a while, you will notice that when you have any disagreement or argument, his first instinct is to dismiss you in a way that makes you feel worthless. He will criticize you in the sort of contemptuous tone that will make you feel dehumanized. When you disagree with ordinary people, you always feel that your opinion matters to them, but with a narcissist, that is not the case. All the things about you that the narcissist claimed to like when he was charming you will somehow turn into negative attributes, and the narcissist will portray himself as a "saint" for putting up with those attributes.

## He Will Hog Your Conversations

Narcissists are in love with the way people perceive them, so they will take every chance to talk about themselves. Whenever you try to have a conversation, the topic will always change, and it will suddenly be about them. It's never a 2-way conversation with a narcissist unless he is trying to manipulate you into thinking he cares about you. You will struggle to hear your views or get him to acknowledge your feelings. When you start telling a story about something that happened to you at work, you will never get to the end of it because he will start his own story before you are done with yours. If you make comments on certain topics of conversation, your comments will be ignored, dismissed, or even corrected unnecessarily.

## He Will Violate Your Boundaries

From very early in the relationship, the narcissist will start showing disregard for your personal boundaries. You will notice that he violates your personal space, and he has no qualms about asking you to do him favors that he has by no means earned. He will borrow your personal items or even money and fail to return it. When you ask, he will say that he didn't know it was such a big deal to you — the point is to make you seem petty for insisting on boundaries that most decent people would consider reasonable.

## He Will Break the Rules

The narcissist will break the rules you set for your relationship, and other social rules, without any compunction. The problem is that sometimes, we are initially attracted to rule-breakers because they seem to be "bad boys" or "rebels," but those traits are, in fact, tell-tell signs of narcissism. A person who breaks social norms is going to break relationship rules because relationships are essentially social contracts. If someone is trying to charm you, but in your first few interactions, you observe that he cuts lines, tips poorly, disregards traffic rules, etc., you can be certain that you are dealing with a narcissist.

## He Will Try to Change You

When you are in a relationship with someone, they will change you in a few minor ways (often unintentionally). However, when you are in a relationship with a narcissist, he will make a deliberate and perceptible effort to change you, and more often than not, it won't be for the better. He will try to break you, and he will try to make you more subservient to him.

You will find yourself giving concession until, in the end, any objective observer can tell you that you are under his thumb. He will cause you to lose your sense of identity so that you end up being a mere extension of him. When you get out of that relationship, you will find it difficult to figure out who you are as an individual because he would have spent the entire duration of the relationship defining and redefining you.

## He Will Exhibit a Sense of Entitlement

The narcissist will demonstrate a sense of entitlement for most of your relationship. At first, he may seem generous and considerate to draw you in, but after that, you will see his entitlement rear its ugly head. He will be expecting preferential treatment all the time, and he will expect you to make him a priority in your life (even ahead of your career or your family). There will be a clear disconnect between what he offers and what he expects, and he will want to be the center of your universe.

## He Will Try to Isolate You

Any narcissist who wants to control you and make you subservient to him understands that you have friends and family as a support system who won't stand by and let him harm you. So, one of the things he will do once he has faked affection and earned some of your trust is, he is going to try and isolate you. He will insist that every time you hang out, you shouldn't bring anyone along. He will make up lies to drive a wedge between you and your friends. He will play into the conflicts between you and your family members to make you lean on them a lot less. If you let him get rid of your support system, he will have free reign, and you won't stand a chance against his manipulation.

## He Will Express a Lot of Negative Emotions

Narcissists trade on negative emotions because they want to be the center of attention. When you are in a relationship with one, he will be upset when you don't do what he wants, when you are slightly critical of him, or when you don't give him the attention he is looking for. He will use anger, insincere sadness, and other negative emotions to make you insecure, get your attention, or gain a sense of control over you. If someone you are dating throws a tantrum over minor disagreements or when you aren't able to give him attention, it means that he has a fragile ego, which is a clear sign that he could be a narcissist.

## He Will Play the Blame Game

This is perhaps the most common indicator that you are in a relationship with a narcissist. He will never acknowledge any wrongdoing, and he will always find a way of turning everything into your fault. When anything doesn't go according to plan, he will always point out your part in it, even if he too could have done something to change the event's outcome. He will never take responsibility for anything, and when he takes action to solve a mutual problem that you have, he will always make it clear that you owe him.

# THE REAL PROBLEMS ASSOCIATED WITH DEALING WITH A MENTALLY UNSTABLE EX

Mental illness is a scary thing for many people, not just those who suffer from it. It's hard to understand how to approach someone mentally unstable, leading to feelings of fear, anxiety, and helplessness.

It's not easy to recognize how to handle a mentally unstable ex-partner. Many people will tell you to walk away, but sometimes it's not that easy. There may be legal obligations or shared children and all sorts of family and community ties that make it challenging to walk away. If you've experienced abuse, there is the added complication that the abusive partner will often rely on you for emotional support—as well as material support—even after they have abused you.

Even if you're not living with your ex-partner, they may still be a significant part of your daily life. If that's the case, you need to look at what is best for all parties concerned. You need to decide what is best for the children or anyone else who is close to someone mentally unstable.

Look at your own needs as well as those of your ex-partner. The bottom line is that it's best to be in a situation where no one is being hurt. If you can't do this, then break contact. Break all links with your ex-partner completely if at all possible. You can call the police if you are physically threatened or if your ex-partner breaches any court orders or injunctions.

However, sometimes it's not possible to be completely disconnected. Sometimes the children are involved, and occasionally other family or friends are too. Whatever the case, it's essential to establish a good relationship with anyone who might be affected by your ex-partner's mental instability. It can help to create a plan and a plan for action that can address any concerns that might arise.

Everyone will deal with a mentally unstable ex-partner in their way and at a pace that suits them. You need to think about some points before making any decisions. Some of these things are about practicalities, including medical and legal issues. However, some of the considerations are no less important but are about your emotional well-being and that of your ex-partner and other people who might be affected by what you do.

The legal issues can be complicated. If the mental illness has been formally diagnosed, then you will have some legal rights in this respect, but these will vary depending on things like where you live and any court orders or injunctions that have been issued.

In terms of practicalities, it is important to consider where your ex-partner is living. You will need to decide whether they're in a position to look after themselves, not just financially, but also with things like food and shelter. If you can't take care of them yourself, it is best to try and get someone else to do so. It may be that the person with mental illness can make their own decisions or arrange somewhere suitable for themselves. If that's the case, then you don't have any responsibilities in this respect.

If you have the right to see the children without your ex-partner present, it may help to arrange something like this well in advance. This way, you can give yourself time to think about how you will deal with the situation before you get there.

It's very important to consider your feelings and how you might react when you come into contact with a mentally unstable ex-partner. You may be frightened or angry, or even sad. Be aware that you will be dealing with a 'raw' situation, and so it's important to keep your own emotions as stable as possible. You can write down any questions you have before seeing your ex-partner so that you can think things through beforehand.

# PERSONALITY TRAITS OF A NARCISSIST AND BORDERLINE NARCISSISTIC DISORDER

People with narcissistic personality disorder are relatively unique. Their personality lends itself to improved social skills and public standing; in the short term, they may appear well-integrated and adapted. However, in a long time, the majority of the following symptoms will become apparent:

## Sense of Self Importance

Most driven people in the world have achieved great things because they believe in themselves and their capabilities. However, once this becomes at the point that this self-importance is exaggerated, and they feel that no one else could be worthy enough to challenge them, their sole aim is for the gratification of self.

## Superiority

No human should feel superior to another; everyone has different skills, and people should be accepted for what they are and for what they are capable of. Differences must be embraced as this is essential to the normal functioning of society. However, someone with NPD will feel superior to all those around them, even if they have not achieved anything to back up this feeling.

This feeling will become so integral with their personality that they will find it impossible to connect on a deeper level. They that only a few people are gifted enough to understand and associate with them.

## Abilities

An extension of this feeling of superiority is the ability to exaggerate their skill levels and achievements. This is partly to ensure that others understand they are superior and partly because they feel more important than anyone else and believe no one would dare to challenge their view of themselves and the world around them. Their conviction and self-belief are often powerful enough for people to follow them without ever witnessing their actual abilities.

# Fantasy

Someone with NPD will spend much of their time dreaming about themselves being rich, famous, or overwhelmingly beautiful. Their fantasies will revolve around others worshipping them for their amazing abilities and achievements and ways in which they will rise to a position of power. They may also create an image of the perfect partner; this can often set the bar too high for any real person to achieve, making it impossible to meet the perfect mate.

# Admiration

A classic trait of someone with a narcissistic personality is vanity. They are generally self-obsessed and believe they are beautiful and, as such, should be constantly praised and admired. This can get to the point where they will quickly feel entitled to this praise and will get enraged easily if they are not receiving it.

# Entitlement

Alongside expecting to be admired, someone with an NPD will feel entitled to success or recognition of their talents and abilities. Failure is simply someone else interfering in their work; they are entitled to success in every field of life and will react extremely badly if this does not happen.
Someone with NPD will expect to be the center of attention at all times; they believe they are entitled to this level of response from others because they are superior.

# Favors

Someone with NPD can't conceive the fact that they are not entitled to whatever they need. They will ask for special favors from anyone they encounter and expect anyone to adhere to their rules and expectations. These expectations are linked with the belief that they are superior to anyone else and are entitled to whatever they want or need.

## Using Others

As other people are seen as inferior, it is difficult, if not impossible, for someone suffering from NPD to see them as individuals in their own right, with dreams and goals of their own. They are more likely to perceive them as a tool that can be used and discarded as required to assist in reaching their aims and goals.

## Needs and Emotions

Someone with NPD does not recognize the needs or emotions of others. This is generally through a physical inability to feel or understand these needs unless their desires are linked with their aims. As they feel superior to everyone else, they do not need to take other people's emotions into account; in fact, they generally do not even realize these people have emotions and needs!

## Envy

Surprisingly, someone with a narcissistic personality is highly likely to be envious of those around them and anything they have, which the sufferer does not. They are also very likely to believe that others envy their achievements, lifestyle, and abilities. They believe this is fitting considering their own highly inflated opinion of themselves. Envy is often difficult to see; it is most commonly displayed through malicious actions to ensure someone else does not have something that the sufferer has not yet got. This can also be recognized as jealously of others and what they have; this is often demonstrated by their hugely exaggerated stories; emphasizing how much better their achievement is compared to one particular person.

## Arrogance

If you genuinely believe that you are better than others and capable of anything you want to do, you are likely to become arrogant. This will then become evident in the way you talk to people and your expectations of their behavior. People with NPD may even come across as haughty as well as arrogant.

# Criticism

Anyone with NPD will not respond well to criticism; the most likely response is to become very angry and defensive; they will attack your argument and your personal beliefs or morals to ensure others devalue your argument and agree with them. The idea that anyone they believe is inferior could be right is impossible to grasp for a narcissist. Occasionally, the reaction may be to socially withdraw as they are humiliated and ashamed of their inability to override the criticism. This can often lead to a targeted campaign to destroy the credibility of the attacker.

Many of the above features can be attributed to a high level of self-confidence. However, there is a difference between being confident and having a narcissistic personality. Someone suffering from NPD will cross the line regarding what is considered a healthy level of confidence. They are likely to put themselves on a pedestal and genuinely believe their life has more value than the lives of other people.

# Borderline Personality Disorder

People with borderline personality disorder are like narcissists in that they are self-centered, emotionally unstable, and unpredictable. Living with someone who has a borderline personality disorder (BPD) can be like trying to stop a full, boiling pot of water from overflowing. Eventually, it will bubble over, and there is no avoiding it.

Most people with BPD, like narcissists, seek attention and admiration from their spouse as a constant source of supply, and it is only a matter of time when they decide it isn't enough. When this happens, they will most likely seek this same attention outside the marriage or relationship. For histrionics, their most common tactic is using seduction as a means to gain favor with others.

While narcissists and people with BPD may practice the same pattern, they might use a new co-worker, neighbor, or someone unfamiliar with their tactics to "win" them over and use them for their bidding and prop up their sense of entitlement. For many new friends and acquaintances, a person who appears kind and well-intentioned will encourage them to show gratitude and praise, which the narcissist wants in return.

How can you cope with living with someone who has a borderline personality disorder? It's not an easy task, and most people will eventually leave due to the erratic nature of this personality disorder. Learning about the signs to identify BPD is just one step and deciding whether you can continue a relationship is the next stage. It's important to understand how the signs of BPD are incorporated into the context of a relationship, as some symptoms may be minor and others more obvious.

- A person with BPD will avoid living alone and often use their relationships with others to fill a gap in their life. When they first begin dating, they may be ecstatic to fall in love and strive towards pleasing you as much as possible. They may also seek validation and return compliments at every chance, which may seem harmless at first until it becomes repetitive and exhausting. You'll notice their emotional reactions become unstable at times, and the slightest hesitation of validating them can result in feelings of rejection.

- A borderline personality disorder often causes a lot of disruption in life because of their unpredictable behavior; they are unable to keep a job or progress towards meaningful goals in their life. They may put a great deal of confidence in you to help them and expect that love can solve all problems. A person with BPD may start a new job, believing it is the perfect place to work with the ideal employer, only to become angry and disappointed at the slight deviation from their idea of perfect. For example, a supervisor may be reminded to perform a certain task at work and internalize it as criticism. This can propel an emotional outburst and sudden action, such as quitting the job or reacting uncontrollably, where they are relieved of their duties or reprimanded further.

- Since they fear being alienated and alone, they may rely on you more than necessary. Even when someone with BPD is financially secure, their emotional and psychological needs are always in a deficit, and they will never feel completely accepted. There is a good chance that family and close friends may now avoid them due to their unpredictable actions.

- If you date someone with BPD or histrionic personality disorder, they will likely engage in relationships outside of the relationship. You may notice risky tendencies initially, such as dressing in provocative clothing that doesn't fit a specific occasion, such as a formal dinner or meeting your family. They may even flirt or act in a similar matter around your friends, which should be a warning sign.

It's important to evaluate your situation from various perspectives. Ask a trusted friend or family member if they notice anything odd or unusual about someone new you are dating, or a partner, once you secure a relationship. While it's important to discover the signs of anti-social behavior early, it's not always possible, and for this reason, always make sure you remain in close contact with someone you trust, who may be able to help you later.

# WHY YOU SHOULDN'T GO BACK TO YOUR NARCISSISTIC EX AND WHY YOU NEED TO MOVE ON

Once you leave the narcissist, you may feel like a huge weight has been lifted from your chest. You feel like you can breathe again for the first time in a long time. You feel like you have made the right choice for yourself. However, in a short time, you find that the narcissist is back on your doorstep, knocking at your door and asking you to come back or take him back. If he is not trying to get you to go back to him, you may find that you begin to miss him too.

This is only natural and is nothing to be ashamed of—when you have spent a part of your life with someone that you have loved, you are going to naturally miss him. However, you can miss him without going back, and when you can recognize that, you can truly stay away. Remember, staying away is what is in your own best interest. You must be able to stay away from the narcissist to protect yourself. Make sure that you stay away and allow yourself to truly heal into the person that you know that you can be.

There are key actions that you can take to help yourself stay away. It is only natural that you may yearn for that connection, especially the connection you had initially. However, you must resist it to help yourself. These steps will help you keep yourself busy and keep yourself reminded that the abuse did happen, and it is precisely because it happened that you cannot afford to go back to the narcissist.

## Resist the Temptation to Judge and Blame Yourself

As you begin to heal away from the narcissist, it can become easy to allow the blame to shift back to yourself. You may find that you are unhappy with the way things turned out once you have nothing to think about. You may feel guilty, asking yourself how you could let yourself get caught up in a relationship like that in the first place. You may find that you are angry with yourself, wondering how you could not see the red flags when they were right in front of your face. You may feel like you made a royal mistake and that you should have done better. This can lead to you judging and blaming yourself, which will hurt your self-esteem even more.

The narcissist wants you to feel like you were to blame. You may question why you would deserve to escape in the first place. Even if you may not be aware of it as it happens, you may begin to feel like you do not deserve better, and this will lead to your unconscious self-sabotage.

You do not deserve to blame yourself. You were hurt enough by the narcissist—there is no reason to add to it in this manner. Turn your attention to something else that could be productive. Instead of dwelling further, you may be able to find something else that you can do with your time.

## Improve Yourself

When you keep yourself from dwelling, the best thing that you can do is invest it in yourself. When you invest that time in yourself, you can make it productive instead. You allow yourself to learn something new. You take your bad situation and turn it into something good.

What you do with yourself is up to you. No matter what it is, it is symbolic. Your escape from the abusive situation is affording you a chance to better yourself in some way, shape, or form. The narcissist may have intentionally kept you held back, holding you down to make sure that you felt like you could never actually do anything. He may have laughed at your desire to go to school for a new career. He may have told you that you are terrible at cooking when you said you wanted to learn how to bake cakes. He may have told you that you were a failure when you told him that you wanted to start a small business. He had no interest in you bettering yourself because if you had managed to pull it off. Your success would have been a direct threat to him. He would have felt like your success was a challenge, a threat that he was not actually as good as he claimed. He wanted you to avoid bettering yourself for this very reason—he would be able to keep his position of power over you.

This means that when you succeed in bettering yourself somehow, you can acknowledge that you did work hard. You can acknowledge that you did it in the face of adversity, despite the narcissist's negative assumptions. You recognize that you did do something worthy, and you will hopefully have something to show for it, whether that is a degree, a new skill, a business, or anything else. Bettering yourself is never a waste of your time.

## Focus on Self-Care

When you have been in a narcissistic relationship, you grow accustomed to dumping excessive amounts of your time into someone else. You were dedicated to trying to placate the narcissist, who was never satisfied, leaving you endlessly working to do so. When you finally break free, however, you have plenty of free time that will keep you thinking about whether you made the right choice in the first place. After all, the narcissist spent the entire relationship making you doubt yourself—of course, and you would continue to do so at this point.

When you shift that free time that you would usually use to deliberate over your decision onto yourself, you can begin to spend time caring for yourself. This is probably foreign to you after a long relationship—you got used to attending to someone else's needs before meeting your own needs when you were in a relationship with the narcissist. You spent your time making sure that he was satisfied, and you did not spend time taking care of yourself because he was never satisfied in the first place.

Now is the time to pamper yourself. Spend some time focused on yourself. Give yourself a spa day. Spend a mental health day in bed with a book, a carton of ice cream, and a glass of your favorite wine. Do whatever it is that you have always wanted to do for yourself and make yourself feel good. You will give yourself a confidence boost because you will feel clean and whole for the first time in a while.

## Write Down the Reasons You Left

One final way that you can resist returning to the narcissist may be one of the most powerful ones there are. You will be making a list of all of the reasons you chose to leave the narcissist and ensuring that you have them for easy access if you ever feel like you are in a moment of weakness. You will be thinking about the entirety of your relationship with the narcissist, recording what he did, how you felt, and why you should refuse to go back.

Think back to when you realized that you were, in fact, ready to leave. You decided that you were no longer willing or able to accept the abuse in your life. You decided that you deserved happiness and escape from the abusive tendencies once and for all. What was that moment? What happened then that made you come to this realization? Why should you avoid ever returning to the narcissist?

It is best to do this step when you are newly out of the relationship and while the pain of what happened to end the relationship is still fresh in your mind. No matter what that final straw that broke the camel's back was, write it down. Email it to yourself. Scan it and keep it on your phone. Print out a copy and put it in your mirror that you see every morning to remind you of what happened.

When you have had time to begin to recover from what happened and your emotions fade, you are more likely to wonder if you made the right decision, and when that happens, you must have the reason why you left written right in front of you. You should also dictate other abusive tendencies that the narcissist had, what he did, and how it made you feel.

You must then read this; every time you start feeling like returning to the narcissist may not be that bad. When you start to feel like returning would be okay and that you would rather have the narcissist present than not at all, you should spend time reading this letter to yourself. Let it be your sort of guide to understanding why you must avoid returning. It is like your map that shows you clearly what has happened and where you will be going from there. It will keep you grounded and firm in your decision. All you have to do is remember to read it when you start doubting yourself.

# HOW TO DEAL WITH A PERSON WHO HAS NARCISSISTIC TENDENCIES

**E**ach of us tends towards narcissism. There are degrees of narcissism, and most people have normal levels of narcissism as a characteristic.

However, some have very high levels of narcissism characteristics, and you don't know how high and how embedded they are until you've become highly involved in a relationship with them. You begin to notice the qualities that made you attracted to that person are narcissistic features that have become extremely annoying to you.

This person may be a parent, sibling, or other family relatives who have a narcissistic personality. You have to put up with those personality traits but can't challenge or control them. You may have an employer, co-worker, student, teacher, or employee with narcissistic characteristics.

Although there are people who are narcissists, it doesn't mean that they're all terrible. Some people who have elevated narcissistic characteristics can be charismatic, fun to have around, and excel in what they do.

- **Falling for the fantasy and why you shouldn't:** Narcissists are charming and magnetic. They sparkle and draw people into their sphere because they can with their attention-getting personality. They are good at exhibiting terrific confidence. Getting caught up in their sphere can be easy. We think that they will bring about our desire to feel alive and more important. However, it's all make-believe, and it's costly in the long run (Smith M. M., 2018).
- **They won't recognize or fulfill your needs:** Realize that narcissists are looking for admirers, not partners. And, for your information, the admirer needs to show obedience. The only value you have to a person with NPD is someone who tells them how great they are to feed their ravenous ego. You, your feelings, and your desires don't count.
- **Check out how narcissists treat others:** People with narcissistic personality disorder manipulate, lie, disrespect, and hurt others. If they do it to others, they'll do it to you and treat you just the same way and possibly worse because you are the closest person to them.

Don't even think that you're different and will not be treated in the same way. You're not special (nothing personal), and you will be treated the same way as others.

- **Focus on yourself:** Focus on things that you want to achieve for yourself. If you have a talent you want to develop or changes you want to make in your life, this is the path you should follow. Create your reality instead of living in someone else's Fantasy.

- **Don't wear rose-colored glasses:** Stop looking at the narcissist in your life as who you want them to be and see them for who they are. Their bad behavior and the hurt they are causing you shouldn't be excused or minimized. Don't live in denial.
- **Narcissists aren't open to change:** It's a sign of weakness, and they don't want to appear weak; they want to appear superior to others. The real change needs to come when you question yourself whether you want to live with this personality type indefinitely or want to make the changes that will salvage yourself (Smith M. M., 2018).
- **Set healthy and firm boundaries:** Mutual respect and caring for the other person's feelings are based on healthy relationships. However, if you're involved with a person with NPD, they cannot reciprocate these feelings in their relationships. It's not as if they're not willing to return. They're unable to. They don't recognize you, see you, or hear you. You are someone who exists outside of their desires and needs. Your feelings, needs, and desires don't fit in. That being said, narcissists violate the boundaries of others regularly. They not only violate boundaries, but they also do it with a lack of empathy and an absolute sense of entitlement.

Narcissists don't think it's rude and invasive to borrow your possessions without even asking if they can go through your mail and your phone texts, arrive uninvited to your home, steal your ideas, and let everyone think they thought of it, eavesdropping on conversations and volunteering advice and opinions that are unwanted. Some narcissists may think they're your brain and tell you how you think and feel.

- **Develop a plan:** If you have a set of boundaries and have allowed others to violate them, you won't find it easy to retain control. The way to have firmer boundaries is to consider what your goals are and any possible hindrances.

The questions you need to ask to develop your plan, are the most important changes you want and hope to accomplish? In the past, has there been anything that has worked with the narcissist? Is there anything that didn't work? How will your plan be impacted by questioning the balance of power between the two of you? When your new boundaries are set, how will you enforce them?
When you can answer these questions realistically, they will help you make your evaluation of choices and the development of a solid plan, one that should work for you.

- **Unless you plan to keep a boundary, don't set it:** There may be boundaries that you have no problem setting and keeping while there are those you've set in the past, and then let it go and allow the narcissist to roll over it.

In setting your new boundaries, be prepared for the narcissist not to be so happy about them. They will test your mettle and limits in whether you'll stand firm by them or not. Let the narcissist know that along with the new boundaries there will be consequences, and be specific in what they are. Backing down is not an option. If you do, you'll be sending a message that you don't need to be taken seriously, and all your boundaries will be in jeopardy.

- **Prepare for other changes in your relationship:** You already know that the narcissist will not be too happy about your new boundaries. They'll feel upset and threatened by any attempts you make to have control of your life, with or without them.

Narcissists are used to having control over you and everyone else. They like to call the shots. They may step up demands in the relationship in other areas to make up for feeling they've lost control over you and the relationship as it was.

- **Taking a gentle approach:** In some cases, some choose not to give up on their narcissist and want to give it a try to preserve the relationship. It's important for you to do so. You need to step lightly and softly. Pointing out their dysfunctional or hurtful actions and behavior, you're doing the worst thing you can do to a narcissist. You're destroying their self-image of themselves and their perfection.

When you let them know that what they've said or done has hurt your feelings, make an effort to give them the message in a respectful, calm, and gentle manner. Concentrate your message on how their behavior makes you feel instead of focusing on their intentions and motivations. They may do their usual routine of responding in their defensive and angry manner. Try to keep calm. If you see you can't continue the conversation, walk away, and see if you can revisit it at a later time. (Smith M. M., 2018)

- **Try not to take things personally:** Narcissists always deny their mistakes, shortcomings, and inferiority complex to protect themselves from feeling shame and inferiority to others. One way they do this is to cast their faults on others.

One of the most upsetting things to feel is to be accused of something that's not your fault or has negative traits that you do not possess applied to you as your personality characteristics. Try not to take it personally as difficult as it can be for you. It's not about you.

- **The narcissist's version of who you are is wrong:** A narcissist's world is not one of reality, including how they view other people. Undermining the self-esteem of others is almost sport to them. Don't allow them to twist who you are and into someone you're not or thrust their blame game on you. Refuse to receive or accept any blame, criticism, or excessive responsibility. Those are negative vibes and accusations the narcissist can keep.

- **Don't bother to argue with a narcissist:** Usually, when we argue with a person who is not a narcissist, there is usually a back and forth and points made on both sides. The key here is that the other person acknowledges and hears you.

When you're being attacked by a narcissist, your natural response is to defend yourself and argue rationally to prove to the narcissist that they are wrong. However, they don't hear you regardless of how rational your argument is. Fighting with them is a waste of breath. Just let the narcissist know you don't agree with the evaluation and move one. Don't entertain the argument if they try to revive it. To control discontinuing the argument, let them know you are over and out.

- **Let the narcissist know that you know yourself:** Having a strong sense of self is annoying to a narcissist. They see that if you have that sense of self, their insults and projections of their personality traits and weaknesses won't work. When you know yourself, your strengths, and your weaknesses, it is much easier to ward off any insults and criticisms that are unfairly leveled against you.
- **Discard the need for approval:** This goes hand in hand with knowing yourself. You need to draw your strength and approval of yourself from your own opinion and truths that you know about yourself. It's really imperative to detach and let go of the narcissist's opinion of you and any wish to appease or please them at your own expense.

This is a boundary that you not only put in place for the narcissist to abide by but one that you should promise to keep for your self-respect and honor of who you are.

- **Look Elsewhere for Support and Purpose:** Let's get real about a relationship with a narcissist. If you decide to remain in such a relationship, you need to be honest with yourself. You have to understand what you can fully and can't expect from them.

A narcissist isn't magically going to change into a person who will truly value you. That means you will need to seek out personal fulfillment and emotional support elsewhere. Cultivate new friendships—Some narcissists want to control the people in their lives by isolating them. If this situation is one that you are in, you need to take the time to rebuild any friendships that fell away because of the isolation or begin to develop new relationships.

# HOW TO DEAL WITH A PSYCHOPATH

**D**ealing with a psychopath is not going to be easy—at least, not at the beginning. Did we not see that a psychopath follows no logic when deciding to act? This is not a person you can reason with. In any case, from what we have already seen, a psychopath is a master of manipulation: they are always using lies and pretense to influence the way you behave towards them.

With that said, you can reduce the damage they bring into your life or even avoid getting entangled in their lives in the first place.

## Great Principles that Can Help

### Seek Professional Assistance

A psychopath is one guy who can transform you from one confident and flamboyant person to a withdrawn and unhappy person. This emanates from the tendency of the psychopath to drum negatives onto you. To psychopaths, you are the cause of things going wrong in their lives; and sadly, you seem vulnerable enough to believe it. That unwarranted blame then gets to seep into your skin, your heart, your mind, and the whole of you, messing with your personality a great deal.

That mess that has occurred in you as a person can only be undone with the help of a professional. Luckily, psychologists have studied the behavior of psychopaths, and your situation will not be new to them, however serious you think it is. They will, hence, show you how to reclaim your person, as you have already been molded into someone else without you realizing it.

One thing you should know is that just as great professionals can be psychopaths, so can great professionals and people of means fall prey to psychopaths. In short, you need not fear stigmatization; it is not your fault you are a victim of a psychopath.

### Beware: Psychopaths Try to Make You What They Want

Psychopaths want you to look up to them as your ultimate solution to problems like only they can bring happiness into your life. Well, they messed you up in the first place, and it would be great if they could restore your being. However, they want you as their victim forever—bidding them every call. For all practical purposes, there is nothing more they want but to enslave your mind.

Suppose you take the example of cult leaders. In that case, it is easy to understand the manipulation of the psychopath and how, as the victim, you end up locking everyone else out of your life, particularly family and friends. See how one Warren Jeffs led a cult that practiced polygamy and abused underage girls and boys. Gladly, in this case, some bold victims testified down the line, and Warren got a jail term in Utah, US, in 2007. Once you are aware of how psychopaths work, you can see the manipulation for what it is and stand firm, refusing to succumb to their control. If you had a plan to use a certain route, for example, and you refused to get influenced and alter the route, the psychopath realizes how difficult it will be to get you trapped. Often, that will be the end of that attempt as the mouth of the psychopath is always watering, longing for easy prey. If you are informed and wise in the ways of the psychopath, they will give up and leave you alone.

## Do Not Be Generous with Information

Ever heard of the analogy of someone throwing you the rope with which you hang yourself? That is what happens with psychopaths and their pretentious concern for you. They use that feigned concern, sometimes in a dramatic way, to get information out of you. And then it is hallelujah as the psychopath uses the same information to manipulate you.

If, for instance, you volunteer information that you had some misunderstanding with your mum or dad, the psychopath takes that information and paints a picture of parents who loath you. Therefore, the psychopath will pose as your savior. And down the psychological decline, you begin, as you become easily brainwashed to review all your other relationships to end them. Every bit of detail that comes out of your mouth is fodder for the psychopath. If the psychopath is in your life in a way that you cannot ignore chatting with them, keep to facts when chatting, and avoid showing your stand or opinion. This is because it is your stand that psychopaths are out to change to suit them.

## Understand the Weaknesses and Strengths that You Have

Why is this important? It is important because the psychopath is already registering your weaknesses to capitalize on them. The same psychopath takes note of your strengths to know the best way to circumvent them when trying to manipulate you.

For instance, right now, you may not need to think long and hard to identify someone who has gone all out to misuse your generosity. Just because you make donations to the less fortunate and do shopping for your mum is no reason for someone else to manipulate you into buying stuff for them. That is the stuff psychopaths are made of.

## Heed Your Instincts

If your senses tell you something does not feel right about someone, find your way out. If you are still strangers, make haste and purport to have company around or do something just as dramatic; get out of wherever you are and lose that company.

And in case it is a budding relationship you are having with someone, and your system keeps ticking caution, nip it in the bud before it turns out to be damaging to your person, your life, and the people around you.

## Drop All Contact

If you feel you have been entangled with a psychopath and want to sever contact, suppress your urge to call even once in a while to say hello. Do not even send text messages. If you send those, the psychopath will jump onto that concern you have just shown and use it to resume the journey of manipulation.

One thing you need to know is that psychopaths have nothing of quality going in their lives. In fact, they are idle for the most part, and when they are busy, it is in the business of seeking out victims. Of course, to them, anyone who is not their victim is their competitor.

## Do Not Bother Trying to Change the Psychopath

When it comes to psychopaths, the solution is to part ways. Trying to reform them usually worsens the situation. And if you introduce them to a specialist, they leave there wiser and more cunning than before. They do not reform; they only get more ammunition for manipulation.

After all, we are talking of people who are full of themselves, selfish, and with no conscience. What professional can really help with a conscience? That is a really tall order.

## Do Not Carry Any Guilt

It would be unfair to you to beat yourself up for falling victim to the psychopath. You were busy leading your normal life, and you had many people to interact with in a positive way when along came the psychopath unleashing all the manipulation. Since you are a normal human being, you hardly realized that this person was not normal but a psychopath and a leech.

### Get Informed

The more information you get regarding the thinking and behavior of a psychopath, the better your recuperation process. You will come to terms with the reality that it is not that difficult to fall victim to a psychopath when you have not come across one before. You can easily get apt information from books on psychopathic tendencies, videos, and also, movies.

## And How Will Information on Psychopathic Tendencies Help?

**You will understand:**

- What characteristics of yours made you vulnerable at the onset
- The whole process and how the charade continued the whole time
- The tactics the psychopath used to keep you toeing the line
- The reason you fell for those tactics

Once you understand the whole process, you will feel a sense of freedom. And that is the only way you will be able to undo the psychological damage done to you by your experience in the hands of the psychopath.

### Set Your Conscience Free

It is easy for you to ask yourself why you could not see the manipulative tendencies, which brings about a great weight that comes from blaming yourself. You need to stop blaming yourself for not seeing through the psychopaths.
Now that you are not a psychopath, how would anyone have expected you to have identified one on the spot? The personal blame is not warranted, and you need to allow yourself a fresh start.

# HOW TO RESPOND TO THE EX

I t may be complicated at first but divorcing a narcissist is worth it. Isn't this a statement you tell yourself every day!? It plays in your mind like a mantra, the self-affirmation reminding you that going in the right direction will be worth it in the end. It should be so easy — why stay with someone who has no empathy, care, or kindness towards you and who wants to see you suffer? Yet, it is not as easy as it seems, hence why you need to repeat statements such as this.

This is one detail that many people don't tell you when taking steps to divorce a narcissist. You need mantras or affirmation-like statements to keep you on course, remind you that this is in your best interests and that it will be worth it in the end. The psychological, mental, and emotional abuse and trauma you have suffered are real, and regardless of how many times you have been gaslighted or made to appear crazy, in the wrong, or losing the plot, you know the truth in the core of your cells. Being with a narcissist is entirely detrimental to your health.

Luckily there are many steps which can be taken. A covert narcissist is precisely this: covert; still in the shadows of their own manipulations, delusions, and shady: hurtful character. They are not (yet) in the open or publicly acknowledged, and is this because you have not yet made the decision to allow them to be seen in their true light? Taking a stand and choosing, with your own free will, inner strength, and sheer conviction, that you will no longer allow yourself to be abused, victimized, or manipulated allows your partner to be seen, and for you to subsequently finally take the steps necessary to be free from their abuse.

Of course, all of this is something you know, so see these words as a reflection of your own psyche and conscious mind telling you exactly how it is. The fact that you are reading this and have chosen, consciously, to align with your true self and leave your narcissistic partner for good implies that you are already well on course. This is confirmation, and you are heading in the right direction! You are strong beyond measure.

## Divorcing a Narcissist: Stop Reacting!

The reaction is not the same as the response. When you respond to someone or something, you provide space, wisdom, and awareness to connect on a mature and responsible level. Responding allows for authenticity, calmness of thought, and clarity in communication. Yet, reacting is something completely different.

The key to your narcissistic partner's success is in your reaction. They need people to become emotionally entwined and engaged with their stories. There is no exchange if there is no reaction—no one is appeasing or empowering them. Power is a great word to be aware of here. The reaction provides a narcissist's empowerment or, more accurately, a false sense of empowerment. Causing pain, hurt, and manipulation to others is not empowerment. Regardless, reacting provides the sustenance that a narcissist needs, so the best way to heal and begin your own journey of empowerment is to stop reacting and start responding.

## Things to Be Mindful of How You May Be Reacting!

Your partner attempts to provoke a reaction, and you allow it. Instead of taking a moment to slow down, be calm inside and recognize the intentions of causing destruction, chaos, and harm, you play to their manipulations. Thus, a vicious and highly repetitive cycle can begin and continue for hours or even days on end. The key is to detach and not get caught up in their games. It can be easier said than done. However, the tips and techniques for effective response below can really help with this.
'Snide remarks.' at this stage, your partner should know you very well and therefore understand your triggers. Snide remarks or specific comments are a very effective way to get a reaction from you and subsequently enable them to continue in their ways.
'Awareness goes where energy flows!' If you don't give your attention, time, or energy to something, how can it perpetuate? The answer is that it can't. The intentions and motivations of your partner require energy and attention. Otherwise, they are formless. Watch out for the signs. Say you have been with your partner for a while. You will know the signs of when they are going to begin their games. If they are bored or displaying signs of frustration, stimulation, or boredom, this is a sure warning that you will soon become their target for their stimulation. A narcissist needs that 'spark' to feed their egocentricity, self-centeredness, and feelings of self-worth. Without it, their illusions start to crumble down, and they have no choice but to look within, seek help, and ways to change, which are, of course, very rare for a narcissist.
If you feel yourself becoming stressed, anxious, nervous, or heated inside, these are a sure signal that you are on the edge of a reaction. Unlike in partnerships where narcissism is not present or a key theme, and where most people are allowed a few moments of blowing off steam or showing weakness, in this relationship, you are not provided the patience, compassion, or support necessary.
This means that even when or if your partner does happen to be in a serene, kind, or non-narcissistic space, you may, unfortunately, spark them with your own reactive behaviors. It is exceptionally rare for a true narcissist to see you becoming upset or worked up on your own accord and not use it as a chance for drama or further manipulation.

# A Deeper Look into Divorce and Reaction

Divorce is a serious thing. The process inevitably means that you have decided to part ways, restart your life, and take back your individual resources, belongings, and physical necessities. Your partner's entire identity is merged in the reality that they can feed off you, use you as their hidden and subtle yet powerful support system, and bounce off your kindness, empathy, and positive attributes.

Once you started responding, this destroys their world. They no longer keep up the facade once you make the decision that their actions are not acceptable. This can only happen when you begin to respond.

# How to Start Responding

The true response begins when you start to slow down and become an observer of both your own thoughts and feelings and your partner's. This is best achieved through meditation and mindfulness. The significance of these two self-help methods cannot be overlooked. They are both extremely powerful in helping you to live your best life, be free from narcissistic abuse or targeting, and start responding.

## Meditation

Why is engaging in meditation one of the best ways to learn how to respond and thus change the way you perceive and feel about the situation? Because meditation allows you to detach from overactive thoughts and feelings, further becoming the observer. When you observe, you are not caught up in the emotions or drama associated with your partner's intentions. You can calm your mind, control your feelings and responses, and feel more peaceful within. Clarity of mind and thought can also result, and you generally become more insightful, patient, wise, and loving with meditation.

## Mindfulness

Linked to meditation is the power of mindfulness. It allows you to become more mindful or conscious, which means embodying a higher awareness and level of integrity. You won't want to react when you start to integrate the lessons and vibration of mindfulness, as you will not want to lower yourself to such levels.

There is an innate dosage of eloquence, self-respect, grace, and personal integrity associated and developed with mindfulness, and your viewpoints and perspectives will change for the better. Any action or behavior of your partner can be met with greater conscious reaction and response. Moreover, you will start to feel good about the situation, regardless of how testing it is, and will see the positive.

In essence, mindfulness can help you see the light and recognize that your mind is a powerful tool. You are not responsible for your partner's thoughts, behaviors, or/actions, but you do have control over your own.

# HOW TO DETERMINE WHETHER TO STAY IN A MARRIAGE/RELATIONSHIP OR TO LEAVE

**W**hether or not you feel like you have been the victim of narcissistic abuse, being in a relationship with a narcissist is not without its challenges. It may lead to an unhappy end, or rather, it could lead to you staying in it, even when it contradicts who you are as a person and your dreams and goals of successful relationships and a happy life. Whatever you are feeling at this moment, letting go of your relationship may not feel like your first choice, and that's okay.

Spend more time reflecting on the issues in your relationship from a more objective standpoint for a little longer about letting go and moving on.

For some readers, there is no question that it is time to pack up and go. It will depend on a person's wants, needs, and ability to be honest with what is going on in their marriage or partnership. Understand the dynamics of your narcissistic partnership after you have identified that you are in one.

Moving forward can be a challenge. Many people will struggle with ending this type of relationship, mainly due to the reality of narcissistic abuse and emotional manipulation. It is about who you are, what your experience is, and what is going on that will help you understand the best choice forward for you.

This will help you identify when it might be good to leave a narcissistic relationship and how to put an end to it so that you don't keep coming back to it and repeating the same patterns repeatedly. A lot of that experience requires getting help and support and eventually a period of recovery from the narcissistic relationship so that you don't end up with the same type of person again, repeating the patterns in an entirely new relationship.

## When and How to End the Relationship

Trying to change a narcissist and help them work on growth and transformation will not get you very far. If you are trying to stick around and make it work, the best possible advice is to focus on their positive qualities. Even if your narcissist claims that they want to change, there will be little effort put forth and very little gain. They aren't going to be able to offer a change in the way you need or hope, and you will most often find yourself alone emotionally. You want to heal them, but only they can heal themselves, and so you might be waiting for a long time for them to figure that out.

The time is right for you to leave if you have undergone any emotional, mental, or physical abuse. Suppose you have identified serious cycles of manipulation or narcissistic issues that never change. In that case, you are sacrificing your power, integrity, success, and desires, or if you feel like you are being taken advantage of regularly to support someone else's fantasies of who they are. There are many ways that narcissism from within your relationship can affect your quality of life, personal views, self-worth, and more, and it is not worth it to stick around, hoping that your partner will change and be more what you need. They don't care about what you need. They will only ever care about what they need.

If you have tried for a long time to help your partner identify their issue and help them "heal" their problem to no avail, then it is time to let go and move on. It is important to recognize that you can never heal someone for them; they have to do the work to heal themselves. Being a supportive partner is always a good thing. Still, suppose you are familiar with how your support patterns have enabled your narcissistic partner to stay in their preferred role and behavior patterns. In that case, you need to admit that you are at the end of the rope to heal on your own and find a happier lifestyle.

The stages of detaching from your partner can go on for a while as you begin to identify the issues and start to pull away, changing your role in the situation and recognizing your readiness to end things. It can be uncomfortable for your partner, who will make it uncomfortable for you as a result, and so understanding some of the stages that you will likely go through will help you prepare for moving on.

## Detachment from a Narcissist: Stages

### First Stage

You stop accepting blame, guilt, or shame in your relationship. You begin to resurface and "wake up" to what has been going on. In the first stage, you are "seeing" more clearly all of the patterns, the covert and subversive ridicule, and all of the tools of manipulation to push you away and punish you, and then pull you back in and adore you. This is the stage of awareness of the problem and the first shift and changes in the situation.

## Second Stage

You may still have feelings for your partner at this point, even a seriously deep love bond. The desire to please them will begin to be replaced with the feeling of anger and even resentment. They consistently and continuously demanding of your admiration, adoration, and pleasing them. The love may still be there, but you are not so "naïve" anymore.

### Signals of the Second Stage

- Your partner lies no longer affect you and feels obvious and pathetic.
- You are no longer succumbing to the manipulation tools.
- You regain a sense of self-worth and feel you deserve to be treated better.
- You will begin to fight for yourself more and will create more conflict with your partner.
- You begin to regain and rebuild your self-confidence and self-esteem.

## Third Stage

Your confidence is being reborn, and you are feeling better about yourself and your choices. You may have already joined a support group or started to see a counselor help you grow and feel more emotionally and mentally empowered. You can better focus on your wants and needs and start seeing how life would be if you are not involved with your narcissistic partner.

### Signals of the third stage

- You cannot stand to be around your partner.
- You no longer feel an obsessive love or strong love bond.
- If they begin to push your buttons or act inappropriately, you will either have no reaction and not care or retaliate and lash out against them.
- Enjoying more time with friends, in support groups, engaging in classes or group meetups that support your interests
- You will start to make decisions to support yourself without concerning yourself with your partner's preferences or interests.
- You will begin to make your move to let go and move on by planning to get out and getting your ducks in a row.

## Fourth Stage

This is the end of the relationship when your focus becomes facing your future without your partner. At this point, you may have cut the cords, moved out, separated, begun the divorce proceedings, etc. This is the stage when you will have cut them off and out of your life and when you can begin to feel new and like yourself again. You will not want anything to do with your partner, and in some cases, you may have to maintain some contact.

# RECOGNIZING HIDDEN EMOTIONAL AND PSYCHOLOGICAL ABUSE TRAITS AND FINDING HEALING FOR THEM

**Y**ou have been to hell, but how do you get back from there? What does your future look like? Can you destroy the trauma bond that you have become addicted to? Can you ever feel like yourself again?

These questions and more can come to the surface when you first manage to break away from your abuser. Life can seem strange and scary. You will feel yearnings to go back to your old relationship, even though you know all the reasons you should not.

For some people, the road to healing is not just about healing themselves, but they also want to find healing in their relationships and for their partners. There is a way to do this as well—it is hard and trying but not impossible. You can get there with work, dedication, and leaning on others for help.

Do not make the mistake of trying to do all of this on your own. There is no shame in seeking help. If you ask yourself: "Well, what is next for me?"

## Where Do I Go from Here?

### How Can You Heal After Being Subjected to a Relationship with a Narcissist?

Your recovery is an involved process. You know what abuse looks like from a narcissist, and you have explored the details behind the narcissist's history. You have learned who the narcissist is, what their masks are like, how they manipulate you, and in essence, you have discovered what has been happening to you. This can be a lot to take in at first. But you need to learn these signs and identify the signals so that you can prevent yourself from being placed back into a situation like this.

Healing takes time and effort. You need to learn about yourself before you can try and heal the damage that your narcissist caused. For example, you need to learn about your childhood trauma that has made you susceptible to caring for a narcissist. Understand also how to create and establish boundaries that we need to make others adhere to. You need to understand that you are also accountable for your actions and the behaviors that you portray. These are all things you will learn on your path to healing so that you can find peace and a way forward after your traumatic ordeal.

Yes, the narcissist's behavior was heinous, but you need to analyze the other half of the equation—yourself. Ask yourself hard to answer questions like why you stayed and why you allowed the ill-treatment to go on for so long? Do not ask these questions to blame yourself but to analyze your behaviors. You are not to blame for the situation, but you need to understand how and why you stayed in an abusive situation. Or even why you continue to stay if you have not left your narcissist.

If your narcissist fails to get help, you need to make peace with the fact that they will never truly take accountability for the emotional turmoil they put you through. This is merely due to the way their mind works. You need to find closure for yourself without expecting it from your partner or ex-partner.

You will go through several stages on your journey to healing.

### Stage One

### *Victim*

When you first learn of everything you have been subjected to and realize that your partner is a narcissist, you will probably feel victimized. This is because you are coming to terms with the betrayal that your narcissist has created. The feelings that you have pent up inside you that add to this feeling of victimhood are:

- Hurt
- Denial
- Rejection
- Confusion
- Shame
- Victimization by family members or friends that say you are crazy for your beliefs about your partner
- Anger at your narcissist
- Anger at yourself for not realizing or knowing
- Anger over the love that you gave
- Anger over the time that you spent in the narcissist's cycle
- Fear of what your next step will be
- Fear of being in an unfamiliar new reality

- Feelings of abandonment
- Feeling lonely

These feelings will run through your mind as you break ties with your narcissist or seek to change the behavior. It is a process as you have also become addicted to the way they treat you.

Your next step in this stage is to arm yourself with knowledge. You need to be prepared to learn about your narcissist and yourself. Once you have looked introspectively into your past and feelings, you need to study what factors made you their target. How did you allow them to creep into your life, and how did you become accustomed to the abuse? Write these questions down and try your best to answer them objectively.

## Stage Two

**Survivor.**

Once you get through your feelings of being a victim and the shock of realizing what was happening to you, you will begin to feel like a survivor. You have a mental shift during this time. Your feeling will change towards:

- Rebuilding your life
- Seeking out a counselor
- Being unwilling to forgive your narcissist
- Try to find your way back to your old self
- Navigating through your issues of trust
- Learning how to understand yourself and participating in self-care
- Re-evaluating and changing friendships as necessary
- Your anger diminishes
- You feel hope
- A trigger could make you feel angry or depressed
- Discovering your trauma from childhood
- Creating awareness for the flags of a narcissist

You will need to actively work toward instilling change in your life at this point in your healing. This is where the real legwork of your recovery begins.

Before you do anything, you need to learn how to create boundaries and set limits that you do not want someone else to cross. This is how you begin taking your life back. Once you have established your boundaries, stop hiding.

Get back into routine and habits with your friends and family. Go out and have fun. Rediscover the freedom and joy that life can give you.

You might be struggling with forgiveness. That is not unusual, but you need to work on it. Your forgiveness is a pivotal step in your recovery. This act is not for your abuser but entirely for you. You need to let go of their control over your emotions and actions.

## Stage Three

### *Surviving and Thriving*

This is the stage where you have laid the foundation for your healing, and now you need to continue to build and work on it. You might feel troubled during your recovery, and some initial feelings of anger and resentment might surface.

- Feelings of anger toward the person that abused you
- Unable to shake the emotions from your past
- Shame and embarrassment at having been the victim of a narcissist
- Lack of concentration in your life at work or even when part of a group setting
- Feeling like you cannot move forward into your new life
- Feeling bitter at the idea of forgiving your abuser
- Conscious of what other people might think as they see you struggle to move on
- Desire to move on and create dreams and live in freedom

It isn't easy to process what happened to you and to clear your mind to move forward. There are ways you can take to reinforce your recovery during stage three.

You need to refocus your perspective. You must learn about the dangers of keeping your emotional attachment with an abuser you left. There is the power to be found from releasing your abuser. Your focus needs to be on your recovery, not on the narcissist.

Find the self-confidence you are missing. There was you before your narcissist grabbed hold of you. Your confidence will help you move forward. Through your confidence, you should strive to learn to love yourself. By loving yourself completely, you can wash away the chaos and anxiety your narcissist left with you.

Change is important. With these steps, you can reclaim some of your former self back yet also forge a new identity for yourself. Learn to be mindful. Place yourself in every moment and be awake and active during it. As you practice mindfulness, your focus will keep bringing you to present moments, and you will be able to let go of the memories that keep surfacing from the past.

When you are ready, you can start building up healthy relationships. If you have let go of friends during your recovery, try to cultivate new and authentic relationships that offer you support.

# SOLUTIONS AND STRATEGIES YOU CAN ACTUALLY USE AND APPLY IN ALL RELATIONSHIPS TO RESOLVE CONFLICT

Conflicts can be resolved in relationships, but they must be committed to the process. If either or both couples are not willing to resolve the conflict, then the relationship may end. There are steps couples must take to resolve conflicts in the relationship.

## Be Willing to Discuss

The first step is for couples to be willing to come together to trash pertinent issues to resolve them. But the situation whereby either are not ready to talk resolving the conflict won't be possible.

Dialogue is the way out of any conflict. The more you and your partner are willing to discuss issues affecting the relationship, the better the chances of resolving them. The couples involved must do well to make the discussion yield even when an arrangement is made. Both must do well to observe the following rules while the conversation lasts.

Each partner should turn to talk and express their grievances. Both must not be speaking at the same time. Otherwise, understanding will not be achieved, and another quarrel may start.

Each partner must listen with keen interest when one person is talking. Phones must be off, and anything that could distract should be put off. Any attempt to interject when one is talking should be with consent.

Avoid argument and use of insult words during the reconciliation conversation. You can show yourself and your views without ever insulting your partner or making him or her feel bad. Choice and usage of words must be selective and politely spoken with respect and dignity.

## Be Objective

As you talk with your partner, you need to be objective. By this, you should try to see the issues raised from your partner's point of view, not just your own opinion. Failure to do so will render the discussion fruitless. Remember your partner is human and that you can't always be right in everything. Try to spot out what your partner is saying that you are guilty of. Read through the lines when your partner is talking to understand the real issues.

## Admit Your Fault

What happened in the garden of Eden that tore the first marriage apart was that both Adam and Eve never admitted their fault before God. The man passed the blame for the error to his wife. The wife passes the blame for her mistake to the serpent. Who will the serpent blame? The blame game right from the beginning did not resolve the problem in the first marriage. Instead, it will scatter it. They were thrown away from the garden of Eden. In any conflict, both will be at fault in one way or the other. To resolve the conflict, both must acknowledge their mistake before God and each other. Only then the reconciliatory steps can be productive.
If you genuinely love your partner and have fate in the relationship, put your ego aside and admit you were all along wrong. You lose nothing when you do so. It is a show of maturity and forthrightness to admit your fault, which will begin the healing process in your relationship.

## Apologize

One of the magic words that can heal and resolve conflict in your relationship is to say, "I am sorry," short but powerful, but unfortunately, most people won't say it to their partner out of pride. If you admitted your fault, it would be natural to apologize. If you need to kneel to apologize, do it to save your relationship from collapsing.

## Forgive

Learn to forgive your partner. If you don't forgive your partner, then you are not ready for peace. Forgiving your partner not only resolves the conflict but also heals you physically, emotionally, and psychologically. It will restore you and your relationship. It is hard to forgive but is also possible by the help of God to forgive. Mutual forgiveness must take place for conflict to be resolved. Let the offense go off your heart. You are better off when you do so.

## Shift Ground

Parties must be willing to shift grounds on issues discussed. A situation whereby you still hold to your stand won't help the reconciliatory process. The win-win approach must be adopted. A little bend here and there between the parties involved is what will mend the broken bridges in the relationship. Don't insist it must go 100% your way. Be considerate and flexible in your decisions so that you and your partner can resolve the conflict and get along well again.

## Make Renewed Commitment to Your Partner

After apologizing, forgiving, and shifting grounds, then the last step is to make a renewed commitment to your partner. Consider all the right and privileges you deprived your partner of. Verbalize your love for your partner once again and back it up with actions.

A warm embrace, kisses, and holding of each other's hands again will also bring back the lost emotional connection you both had before. Just laugh over everything, and all will be well again.

# HOW TO IDENTIFY ISSUES WORTH FIGHTING, HOW TO FORMULATE THEM TO MINIMIZE ANY CONFLICT, AND HOW TO CHANGE YOUR THINKING STATE TO MAKE IT MORE POSITIVE IN ALL SITUATIONS

Slamming doors, angry words, silent treatment, and a host of other destructive behaviors become the norm if people in a relationship are constantly fighting. Verbal abuse can be just as damaging as physical abuse, so do not delude yourself that since you are just fighting verbally, it means you are not hurting each other. Human beings are naturally emotional. Sadly, it is the people we love who hurt us the most. That is why, in every relationship, conflict will arise.

When two people from different backgrounds and belief systems come together, you will be times that you will disagree. The problem in a relationship is not that there is conflict but rather how the conflict is handled. If you cannot resolve a disagreement without a shouting match or mean to one another, you have an unhealthy way of resolving conflict. You should approach a disagreement to resolve an issue and not impose your will on another person. Absolutes like "never" or "always" can blind you and hinder you from making rational decisions. Avoid making decisions when you are angry. Learn to step back from the situation until you feel calm enough to have a discussion.

## Winning the Battle to Lose the War

Do you want to have a two-hour fight over who forgot to take out the trash? It is not unusual to find couples having blazing rows about the smallest of things. Constant bickering becomes a habit with time, and you start to find that the moments when you are in harmony with your partner become fewer each day. Therefore, it is important to know how to pick your battles.

While you do not want to let your partner walk all over you, working on minor issues is self-sabotage. Living with a nagging partner can be emotionally draining and will drive the other person away. There is a reason some people will leave work and go straight to the bar instead of going home to their partners. Peace of mind is important, and when you cannot get that at home, you start to seek it elsewhere.

Nagging is perceived as criticism for most people, which immediately puts the other person on the defensive. Your partner will probably tune you out the minute you start talking if they have become accustomed to your nagging. Slowly they start to resent you because they feel personally attacked.

You have a better chance of success when you talk to your partner in a friendly and conversational way. Resist the urge to start harping on them the minute they walk in through the door. Wait for the right time to bring up issues, preferably when your partner is relaxed and open to communication. You can avoid aggravating disagreements and conflicts in your relationship by knowing how to disagree without hurting each other.

# Living in Harmony

## Do's

- It is okay to agree to disagree. Not every conflict has to end with both parties coming to the same agreement. On some issues, you will need to be okay with differing points of view.
- Keep the personal attacks out of your disagreements. Discuss the issue, not the person. Refrain from bringing up your partner's flaws to make them feel unsure of themselves or guilt them into agreeing with you.
- Keep your disagreement about the present and resist the temptation to dredge old issues and past mistakes.
- Stop combining all your issues and then linking them all into one big issue. Tackle issues as they crop up and find solutions to each. Do not stockpile all your grievances to be used later as some ammunition against your partner.
- Be responsible for your part in the conflict. It takes two to tango, and both of you have created most of the issues in your relationship. By acknowledging what you may have done wrong, you also encourage others to accept their mistakes. This enables you to resolve and move on from the issue. Stubbornly sticking to your point, even when you know you are wrong, does not resolve disagreements.
- Mind your language. Refrain from using derogatory terms or insults to make a point. Keep the discussion civil and avoid creating animosity. The more you attack the other person, the more closed off they become, and the less likely you will resolve your conflict.
- Make a safe space where you can retreat without needing to discuss the conflict. It can be your bedroom or any other place you feel needs to be spared from the

conflict. This will take some pressure off and give you a safe space and time to handle your emotions.

- Decide upon a time frame where you can discuss the issue and bring it to a close. Avoid revisiting the same issue for days on end. Set aside and decide that you should both reach a compromise by the end of that time and let that issue go. It could be an hour, thirty minutes, or if you feel you need to address the conflict and resolve it.

## Don'ts

- Do not try to win by sticking to your point of view, no matter what. If you view conflicts as a battle for supremacy, it won't be easy to resolve anything.
- Do not view your partner as your competitor. No matter what, remember you are in the relationship together, and you still need to live with each other once the disagreement has passed.
- Do not be manipulative. Using threats, aggression, and manipulation to get your way means that the conflict is not resolved. This means you will find yourself having the same argument you tried to weasel out of sooner or later.
- Do not lie. Even when you are afraid of the outcome, resist the urge to be dishonest or mislead your partner. Be open and truthful.
- Do not let your emotions get into you. Getting angry or defensive will get in the way of effective communication if you need to pause the discussion until you are calm enough to engage constructively.
- Do not use the past against your partner or to justify your actions. Deal with the current issue without trying to make assumptions based on past experiences.
- Do not agree just to agree. Express yourself clearly and avoid saying yes to please the other person. If you make a habit of getting along, you will constantly be discontent because you are trying to suppress your true feelings.

## The Art of Compromise

Compromise doesn't mean giving in to the other person. It means that you understand that you each have needs, and the best way to meet them is to meet each other halfway. Compromise is the willingness to recognize and accommodate the other person's needs without necessarily sacrificing your own. If you are in a relationship and do not know how to compromise, your relationship will be littered with conflicts. Everybody likes to get their way, but when you have decided to share your life with someone, you need to be willing to recognize that your way is not the only way.

When you make compromises a part of how you deal with issues in your relationship, you increase the trust and security in the relationship. Both partners know that even when they have different needs, you will find a way to accommodate each other. This builds harmony in your relationship and enhances the emotional connection.

To be able to compromise in your relationship, you must be adaptable and flexible. See and understand the situation from another person's point of view and change mindset.

## Increasing Empathy for Your Partner

One best way to know someone is to walk a mile in their shoes. This means being empathetic and finding it in yourself to see beyond your own needs and emotions. It is about feeling with the other person and looking at things from their perspective.

You understand where they are coming from when you increase your empathy for your partner. This is crucial in managing conflicts in your relationship. When you are closed off to the other person, your entire focus is on your own emotions, which hinders you from feeling what the other person is going through.

Empathy enhances compassion and strengthens the bond between two people. What can be better than feeling understood and having your feelings validated in a relationship? While empathy is a trait that most people learn in childhood, not everyone can effectively use it.

The following are some tips on how you can increase empathy for your partner.

### Be Present

When you are preoccupied and absent-minded, you cannot pick up on what your partner is feeling. Learn to be actively engaged in your relationship as opposed to just going through the motions. Switch off your phone and other distractions when you are spending time with your partner. This helps you to be present now and enhances your understanding of each other.

### Switch Roles

When you are having a challenging time understanding what your partner's needs are, try switching roles. You can even role play if that will make it easier for you. When you put yourself in someone else's shoes, you get an insight into what they are dealing with and what it is to be them. It is easy to be selfish when you have no idea what your partner is going through. Once you put yourself in their situation, you can get valuable insight into their emotions and needs.

## Do Not Be Judgmental

Even when you do not agree with your partner, disagree respectfully. Refrain from being judgmental or critical. Remember, everyone has had experiences that have shaped the way they see things. Never assume that your point of view is superior. Everyone is entitled to their needs, and the least you can be is open-minded and accommodating.

## Stop Assuming

It is easy to misunderstand others when we assume, we know how they feel or what they need. Ask questions and encourage your partner to express themselves openly so that you clearly understand what they need. Sometimes simply having a deep conversation with your partner can change how you look at them and enhance your ability to identify with what they are feeling. Like we said earlier, nothing beats effective communication in a relationship.

## Go Beneath the Surface

Understand as much about your partner's past as you can. This can help you to understand their emotional triggers. We cannot deny the fact that past experiences influence how we relate to each other. Share your past experiences to deepen your understanding of each other's triggers, tendencies, and weaknesses.

## Be Compassionate

Not everything your partner is feeling must make sense to you. Learn to be compassionate even when you do not understand them. Compassion is part of being human. Acknowledging the other person's fears and insecurities does not hurt you in any way.

# HOW TO IMPROVE MY COMMUNICATION AND PROBLEM-SOLVING SKILLS

I n relationships, problems or disputes consist of any circumstance, incident, or experience that affects or matters to those concerned. Several factors that lead to conflict; some of which include topics such as finances, children and in-laws, personal issues such as self-esteem, beliefs, aspirations, or priorities, or related problems such as the amount of time together versus time alone, support versus power, affection, and communication.

Although there are seemingly endless reasons for conflict, they generally surround all humans' underlying needs, including physical, intellectual, emotional, social, and spiritual. Most significantly, the result is always decided by how we approach and interact with those issues.

The happiest relationships also experience conflicts and problems. It provides opportunities for growth in both personal and relationships if handled well. Many skills can support people seeking to settle disputes safely. Communicating effectively is one of the greatest skills which helps in conflict resolution.

Most people know that we need to communicate to resolve conflicts, but negative communication patterns can often lead to greater frustration and conflict escalation. Consider the following communication challenges:

## Body Language/Voice Communication

The tone is more than the words we choose to use. We sometimes speak our body language and voice tone louder than our words. Shouting, "I'm not angry," for example, is not a very convincing message. If we send a conflicting message where our voice and body language tone is not in line with our message, misunderstandings, and anger sometimes follow.

To surmount this communication challenge, we need to be mindful of what signals our body language and voice tone will convey to others. Speak calmly, give eye contact, a smile if necessary, and maintain an open, relaxed posture.

# Differences in Style

Each of us has a specific way to interact, often based on interactions with our families, history, gender, and several other factors. For example, when our partner's, we can appear to be noisier, outgoing, or emotional. While there's no right or wrong style, our past experiences mostly lead to expectations that are not usually communicated verbally with others, causing relationship tension and misunderstanding. For instance, if we came from a large family that tended to shout for being heard, we might think it's normal to speak loudly. But if our partners came from a quieter family environment, they might be uncomfortable or even scared by an elevated voice.

Discussing our experiences and perspectives will help explain ourselves and others' expectations and help our partner appreciate our point of view. Knowing this knowledge will also help in the process of problem-solving.

# Communication Roadblocks

The roadblocks of communication arise when two people communicate in such a way that none feels understood. Research has identified four especially negative communication styles, sometimes referred to as "the apocalypse's four horsemen," because those interaction styles gradually become lethal to relationships if left unchecked. Criticism, disdain, defensiveness, and stonewalling are such types.

# Criticism Assails the Other's Character or Personality

While it is common to have concerns about the actions of others, it is very different from putting them down as an individual. For example, a complaint may be, "I felt worried when you didn't call me that you were going to be home late." Criticism can be articulated in the same context as, "You're so unconsidered, you never call me when you're going to be late." Criticism focuses on certain behaviors; criticism focuses negatively on the motives and character of the person.

Contempt portrays disgust and disrespect by body language, such as eye-rolling or sneering, or by name-calling, sarcasm, and cutting remarks to the other person.

Defensiveness is an often-natural response to criticism and disrespect by individuals, but it also escalates the dispute.

When we're defensive, we appear to avoid listening to the other's perspective and shut down contact.

Stonewalling withdraws from dialogue and declines to participate in the discussion.

It's the adult equivalent of the "silent treatment" that young kids use when upset. Without touch, dispute resolution is unlikely.

## Additional Examples of Communication Roadblocks Include:

- Order ("Quit making complaints!")
- Warning ("If you do that, you will be sorry.")
- Counseling ("You shouldn't behave like that.")
- Recommending ("Wait a few years before you decide")
- Reading ("If you do this now, you're not going to grow up to be a responsible adult")
- Agreeing, only to maintain the peace ("I think you're right")

Acknowledging these roadblocks and making attempts to communicate effectively will help individuals resolve roadblocks.

# Tips to Resolve Conflict

## Ease the Startup

One of the skills to resolve roadblocks in communication requires a soft start to the discussion by beginning with the constructive, showing gratitude, reflecting on problems one at a time, and taking responsibility for thoughts and feelings. Furthermore, beginning the message with "I" instead of "You" will reduce the defensiveness and encourage positive experiences with others while presenting the issue. For instance, "I want to stay more involved in making money decisions" instead of "you never include me in financial decisions."

## Make and Receive Repair Tentative

Another critical ability in resolving roadblocks in contact is learning how to make and accept attempts at repair. Repair attempts are efforts to prevent an increasingly hostile experience by taking a break or trying to calm the situation. This is critical because we often experience extreme emotional and physical stress when disagreements occur, impairing our ability to think and reason, leading to roadblocks in communication. Taking time away from the dispute to calm down (at least 20 minutes) can help us be more prepared to discuss the problem.

# Speech and Listening Skills Are Important

It takes good speaking and listening skills to resolve roadblocks in communication. There is a method of speaking-listening to help individuals communicate more effectively. Every partner takes turns to be the speaker and the listener.

## The Speaker Rules Include

- Should share thoughts, feelings, and concerns.
- Use the "I" statements when you speak to express your thoughts and feelings accurately.
- Keep statements short of ensuring information does not overwhelm the listener.
- Halt after each short statement so that the listener can paraphrase what has been said to ensure they understand or repeat back in their terms. If the paraphrase is not quite correct, reframe the statement gently again to help the listener understand.

## The Listener's Rules Include

- Paraphrase what the orator says. If vague, request clarification. Proceed until the speaker correctly indicates the message has been received.
- Don't disagree or give an opinion on what the speaker is saying—wait until you're the speaker, and then do it with respect.
- The listener should not speak or interrupt while talking, except for paraphrasing after the speaker.

In each position, the speaker and listener should take turns so that each has an opportunity to express their thoughts and feelings. One can still ask for a time-out. This activity aims not to solve a problem but rather to have a healthy and constructive discussion and consider each other's opinions. Understanding and validating others' thoughts and feelings while we may not always agree with the other's point of view can improve relationships and build on common ground, leading to more effective negotiation and problem-solving.

# HOW TO RECOVER FROM EMOTIONAL ABUSE

Emotional abuse is deeply damaging, and without going through the healing process, you make yourself even more vulnerable to entering into the same type of relationship. You have been violated psychologically, and you will experience anxiety, depression, dissociation, feelings of low self-esteem, low self-worth, nightmares, and flashbacks. It is essential that you seek counseling to assist you in the healing process; however, you can implement strategies in your daily life that will help you move forward.

## Yoga

The effects of trauma live in the body. Yoga is a physical activity and mindfulness that helps to establish and restore balance. Research has proven that yoga alleviates anxiety and depression, improves symptoms of post-traumatic stress disorder in victims of domestic violence, boosts self-esteem, and improves body image. Yoga involves a series of powerful movements that compensate for the feelings of powerlessness that abuse victims are left with.

Dr. Bessel Van der Kolk has spent years studying the benefits of yoga, and he believes that it allows traumatized victims to take back ownership of their bodies. Trauma robs abuse victims of a sense of safety, and yoga helps them reconnect through the use of bodily sensations.

## Meditation

Trauma disrupts the area in the brain responsible for memory, learning, emotion regulation, and planning. Research has found that meditation benefits the same areas of the brain that are affected by trauma, such as the hippocampus, the amygdala, and the prefrontal cortex. Meditation gives abuse victims their psyche back. It heals the brain and allows them to respond to life from empowerment instead of a place of trauma.

Daily meditation practice strengthens the neural pathways in the brain and boosts grey matter density in areas of the brain related to the fight or flight response and emotion regulation. Meditation also allows you to become aware of your need to make contact with your abuser. When victims are not aware of this, they make impulse decisions which usually leads to them returning to the relationship. It will make you aware of your emotions in general.

## Anchor Yourself

In general, emotional abuse survivors have been gaslighted into believing that they imagined the abuse they were experiencing. It is essential that you start anchoring yourself into the reality that you were abused but no longer in that situation. It is common for abuse victims to idealize their relationship and spend time thinking about what could have been if only they were capable of pleasing their partner. Connecting to reality also helps when struggling with mixed emotions towards your abuser. As mentioned, one of the strategies of the narcissist is to show affection and withdraw it, and it is the affectionate side of the narcissist that victims are drawn to. The narcissist seeks to erode their victim's reality, but once you are reconnected with your reality, you can see your abuser for who he truly is.

## Work with Your Inner Child, Self-Soothing

You didn't just happen to fall into an abusive relationship, some deep-rooted issues within you bring you to this point in your life, and they typically stem from childhood. Through therapy, you will discover that some fundamental needs were not met during childhood. In attempting to fill that void, you settled for an abusive relationship. Once you discover what that void is, it is essential that you learn what is required to fill it so that you do not leave yourself vulnerable to enter into another abusive relationship. During the healing process, you will need to be extremely compassionate with yourself because of what you went through as a child, and the abuse you have endured is not your fault. Abuse has the power to open up old wounds that were never healed. The belief system that you have never felt good enough has always been a part of your psyche. Your abusive partner confirmed how you have always felt. When you are healing, it is essential that you change the narrative that is taking place in your mind, which is important in general, but even more so when you are recovering from abuse. Self-compassion can be the most powerful form of compassion, so it is important that you are gentle with yourself during this time.

# Exercise

Whether going for long intensive walks, going for a jog, joining a dance class, or joining the gym, incorporating exercise into your daily routine will help during the healing process. If you don't have any motivation, don't try and do too much at once; for example, you can start by going for a ten-minute walk and then increase it as time goes on.

Exercise lowers cortisol levels and releases endorphins, which help replace the biochemical addiction you developed with your abuser with something that will benefit you. This addiction was formed through chemicals such as cortisol, dopamine, serotonin, and adrenaline, which strengthen the bond with your abuser and form the cycle of highs and lows. Exercise allows you to build a wall of strength and resilience after leaving an abuser. It also helps to eliminate many physical problems associated with the abuse, such as weight gain, sleep problems, premature aging, and a depleted immune system.

# Put Unhealthy Coping Strategies to Bed

You did everything possible to try to keep your narcissistic partner happy and to keep him from flying into a fit of rage. Your days were spent walking on eggshells — you learned how to be silent and submissive, to question your every move, and to start all your conversations with the words, "I'm sorry." You learned how to dodge bullets, avoid landmines, and act as if parts of your dreams, desires, and needs didn't exist.

You learned how to devalue yourself and accept treatment from another unacceptable human being. The anguish you had to go through to experience even a little bit of peace and keep yourself, and maybe your children, safe from harm was astounding. All these terrible things you had to learn were unhealthy, but in a normal relationship, they are not skills that will serve you well; therefore, you must learn new and normal habits that will benefit you in a healthy relationship. Unlearning old habits involves a system of self-monitoring; there are two types, qualitative and quantitative.

- **Qualitative Monitoring:** This involves being attentive to the old habits you are engaging in—what do they look like, and how do they make you feel?
- **Quantitative Monitoring:** This involves counting the old habits that don't serve you to monitor how often you engage in them throughout the day.

Although both types of self-monitoring are effective, quantitative monitoring is most beneficial because, for the first time, you can accurately measure how you are behaving and the triggers that cause these bad habits to resurface. You may have had a slight idea of how bad your problem was, but now you can see it as well as have something to measure your progress by.

# Learn to Love Yourself

It is essential if you will move on with your life and eventually get into a healthy relationship. No one can come along and try to convince you that you are anything less than the best! When you develop a certain level of confidence and self-worth, nothing can shake you. Here are some tips on how to love yourself after an abusive relationship.

- **Get in Shape:** You feel good when you look good! We have already known the benefits of exercise, so looking good is simply a bonus. Make a decision not only to improve your health but to transform your body. Whatever your ideal weight and shape are, aim for that.
- **Change Your Wardrobe:** Once you have achieved your ideal body shape, treat yourself to new clothes.
- **Have Fun Alone:** Take one day out of the week and do something that you enjoy. A lot of abuse victims have difficulty being alone, which is why they are such easy prey for abusers—spending time alone will teach you how to enjoy your own company. Things you could do might include going to the movies, out to dinner, or finding a new hobby.
- **Try Something New:** Do things that you wouldn't normally do. Try something new and crazy like skydiving or bungee jumping. That's a bit extreme, but you know yourself better than anyone else, so you can choose something that you know will add an element of surprise to your life.
- **Go on Vacation:** Even if you don't make it a regular activity, take a vacation somewhere. Go to a country that's completely out of your comfort zone. If you are not brave enough to go alone, invite a friend. Experience a different culture, new food, different activities, and have fun.
- **Journal:** Writing is one way to release any negative emotions you are feeling. It is also a good way of tracking your progress. When you come out of an abusive relationship, you will have more bad days than good ones. There will be better than others; however, after some time, you will notice that your emotions will begin to stabilize.
- **Learn to Say No:** Being submissive is a survival mechanism for women in abusive relationships. You would never dare say no to your partner in fear of what might happen. However, now that you are not in an abusive relationship, it is important that you don't carry this submissive nature into your friendships or feel as if you need to say yes to everyone to please them.
- **Celebrate Accomplishments:** No matter how small you think the accomplishment is, celebrate it. Going through a whole day without thinking about your ex is an

accomplishment and being consistent with your daily exercise routine is an accomplishment. Pay attention to these points and treat yourself for them.

- **Challenge Yourself:** Is there anything you have always wanted to do, but you have never gotten around to doing it? Make a list of these activities and start doing them. You may have always wanted to compete in a triathlon or to get some additional qualifications. Decide that whatever you put your mind to, you are going to achieve.
- **Learn to Trust Yourself:** Before you got into an abusive relationship, your instincts told you that something wasn't right, but you chose to ignore them and pursue the relationship hoping that things would get better. Familiarize yourself with that feeling because sometimes something isn't right, that is how you will feel, and this isn't just about relationships. It's in all areas of your life.

# HOW TO OVERCOME A TOXIC RELATIONSHIP, DEAL WITH AN ABUSIVE EX, AND GET RID OF THE CONTROLLING SOCIOPATH

Toxic relationships let out the worst in you because the other person knows exactly what buttons to push to get you to toe the line. You will find yourself often doing things you would otherwise never consider doing to keep the other person happy. This dysfunction, if left unchecked, becomes a self-repeating cycle that takes over your life.

It poisons you from the inside out. In extreme cases, they may even drive you to coping mechanisms such as addictions to help you process your unresolved issues. This potential for self-harm is one reason why freeing yourself from codependency requires that you eliminate any toxic relationships from your life.

Whether you are dealing with a narcissist who thrives on attention and being the center of the universe or with more covert manipulators, the damage to your self-esteem is hard to repair. Toxic people will come in many different shapes and forms, and you need to identify them by their characteristics. There are warning signs that you need to be on the lookout to identify toxic people and weed them out:

- They like to control you.
- They like to shift blame and never take responsibility for their actions.
- They are overly critical and always trying to find fault.
- They use threats and intimidation to manipulate you.
- They try to gain sympathy by playing.
- They are always complaining.
- They often use emotional abuse to make you feel worthless.

Perhaps the most toxic relationship for a codependent is one with a narcissist. Narcissists have no consideration or interest in other people's feelings or needs. The narcissist is the polar opposite of the codependent when it comes to compassion and empathy.

The following are basic signs that point to a narcissistic personality:

- They lack empathy and never try to meet your needs.
- They manipulate you to get what they want.
- They await you to cater to their every need and whim without question.
- They demand to have the best of everything
- They are continually making you feel inferior

- They have a compulsive need to be the center of attention.

# Tips for Freeing Yourself from Toxic Relationships

## Build Boundaries

Identify your limits and do not compromise on your boundaries. Be very clear on what is and isn't acceptable. Always be ready to enforce the consequence of the other person crossing your boundaries. This means you should be ready to permanently cut off ties with this person if they are unwilling to change.

## Stop Taking Responsibility for Other People's Problems.

The only person whose happiness you are responsible for is you. Stop trying to fix other people's problems. Never feel obligated to rescue or support someone unwilling to take responsibility for their actions.
By trying to fix the other person's problems, you become an enabler and promote dysfunction and codependence in the relationship. People tend to be more conscientious when they know that they will be responsible for the consequences of their actions.

## Discover Your Triggers

Identify the triggers that make you vulnerable to manipulation. Whether you have unresolved issues with guilt, blame, or shame, know what your triggers are. Be vigilant around anyone trying to use these triggers against you. For instance, someone trying to guilt you into doing something you do not want exploits your guilt issues.

## Build Your Emotional Intelligence

Emotional intelligence enables you to manage your emotions effectively. It allows you to stop being reactive to other people and have more control over your behavior and feelings.
Emotional intelligence also increases your social awareness and the ability to recognize other people's motives. It will be easier to see manipulators and energy vampires and give them a wide berth.

## Find Safety and Security in Yourself

When you are secure in yourself, you no longer feel the need to be validated or approved by others. This leaves you free to make decisions based on your needs. Freedom from the need for validation also means that you no longer have to please others to feel loved or accepted. This frees you up to be true to yourself without fretting about other people's opinions.

## Surround Yourself with Positive People

When you build healthy relationships, you will be less likely to get back into dysfunctional relationships. Focus on making new emotional connections with people who share your values. A good relationship will help you get over a bad one that much faster. It will also give you a chance to experience what a good relationship should be.

# PROTECTING YOURSELF DURING A DIVORCE FROM SOMEONE WITH BORDERLINE OR NARCISSISTIC PERSONALITY DISORDER

No divorce in the world is easy; however, divorcing a narcissist can be a terrifying time. You may be worried about the safety and well-being of not only yourself but also your children. If you have decided to divorce your narcissistic spouse, there are some things you need to know. This will lead you to the process of divorce and what you should expect. You will need to find help and create a good defense. We will also know how to deal with a narcissist in court as it is not as cut and dry as other divorce situations.

After realizing that they are married to a narcissist, many people find that divorcing is the best thing they can do for their overall safety and well-being. It is often the best decision for themselves, as well as their children. Making the decision may be difficult, but it will be better for your children and your children at the end of the day. It takes bravery and knowledge to venture down the road of divorcing a narcissist.

There are a variety of stressors that surround a "normal" divorce. People worry about the financial aspect and the difficulty and pain it causes to everyone involved. Many couples won't ever have to go to court, and they will be able to work it out through mediation and other techniques. When fighting with a divorce from a narcissist, things are not only more complicated, and you can almost guarantee a judge will end up being involved. Divorcing a narcissist can become a real mess. People usually work together to stay out of court and find alternatives to the messy process that divorce can entail. When dealing with a narcissist, they will do their best to make things as dirty as possible.

While no one wins in a divorce, the narcissist will strive to feel like they have won. More often than not, when handling divorce, people hope for things to be split down the middle. It includes assets and responsibilities. The narcissist is not going to see it this way at all. They are excellent at playing the victim and will have no intention of meeting you in the middle. They will not take the route of mediation or negotiation.

Their goal will be to be the one seen as being in the right. The truth of a narcissist is anything but truthful.

They will do all means to make themselves look good and sway everyone's opinion, including a judge, to see things from their point of view, even if it is tragically skewed.

The narcissist is also a master game player. They will likely up their game because they are genuinely after a win. They love to hold power, and they do this by keeping other people off-balance. Unfortunately, narcissists tend to be charismatic and charming. It can win favor with a judge or other people involved in your divorce. They will do whatever it takes to wear you down or win the favor of the ones that are making decisions. It makes them dangerous to deal with, especially when kids are involved.

One of the worst actions you can do when dealing with a divorce from a narcissist is to say, "I give up." It is precisely what the narcissist wants. They will ensure this to make it happen. It not only gives them the win but also enables them to feel good about besting you.

They will use this to their advantage with their "friends" and other people to continue making you look bad and making them look like the victim. Stay strong.

You will likely end up in court when divorcing a narcissist as they will refuse to talk on reasonable terms.

One of the reasons that the narcissist prefers court is it helps them avoid accountability. When a judge decides, the narcissist is more comfortable as they don't have any responsibility for turning out. Narcissists don't want to be accountable, so the court system can be blamed rather than whether they win or lose. They also find some illusion of control in putting the decision into the hands of the court.

## Planning and Creating a Secret Account to Fight in Court Against a Narcissist

When dealing with a narcissist, you always want to be proactive. When you are reactive, you are giving them exactly what they want.

There are some things you will certainly want to talk about with your attorney. You should likely also get a therapist involved. When you have been in a relationship with a narcissist, it takes a psychological toll, so does divorce. The two together can break a person apart, so enlisting a therapist is simply a smart decision. It can help you keep your feelings steady and allow you to be productive while working through this challenging journey.

Consulting with a professional can be helpful in many ways. It shows that you are working hard to do your best, and they will be able to give you an unbiased opinion on many things. Remember, you should not be looking for legal advice from your therapist; that is what your lawyer is for. When looking for professional support, finding someone specializing in PTSD and narcissistic traits or narcissistic personality disorder will be your best avenue.

Take your time and do your research. Find a lawyer who will handle the extra difficulties that come with dealing with a narcissist. You may have to talk to several attorneys before finding the right one, staying patient, and not being afraid to ask questions. Eventually, you will find the perfect fit to ensure you use the strategies needed to handle a narcissist. You will also need to take the time to be psychologically prepared. To do this, learn everything you can about narcissism. Learn how to recognize the traits and find the ability to prove that your partner is indeed a narcissist or suffering from a narcissistic personality disorder. You should also seek out a therapist, counselor, or psychologist. As noted, finding one specializing in narcissistic traits and narcissistic personality disorder will be the most advantageous. If they are also familiar with PTSD, you have found yourself a winner in terms of psychological help. Several damages can be done to the partner of a narcissist, and the support of a professional can get you on the appropriate path toward healing and recovering from the abuse you have endured. They can also keep you focused on what is essential.

## How a Specialist Divorce Attorney Can Help You

One thing you need to do when dealing with a narcissist is to let your attorney know. As stated, narcissists tend to present themselves very well, easily fooling someone who does not know them. They are talented at pulling the wool over the general public's eye. By letting your lawyer in on who your ex is, you can both be better prepared with how to deal with them.

At least a low rate will show that the narcissist will show their true nature while working through divorce proceedings, but it is just as likely that they will keep their mask in place. When you offer your lawyer the narcissist patterns and how you have dealt with them, it can explain how to deal with him. It leads us to a perfect point when looking for an attorney; it may be best to ask them right upfront if they have ever dealt with a narcissist. If they have not, you should probably keep looking. When you are in such an unsafe position, making sure the people fighting for you are well-versed in your problems is the best course of action.

# Collect Evidence for the Defense in Court

Keeping good records will also work in your favor. From simple conversations with your narcissistic partner to a list of expenditures, all information is useful. When a narcissist starts to play games with the words said, you want to prove them wrong. Being organized and keeping the storyline straight and accurate is a significant bonus to your side. This evidence can help show the true nature of your soon-to-be-ex and discredit the ridiculous strategies they try and get others to believe.

Maintaining control over your emotions will also be a critical element to your success. The narcissist will try to get you angry to act out, which helps give them more power. Do not allow this to happen. They are doing this on purpose to try and gain power and control. Do your best to minimize communication as this will leave less opportunity for you to lose your cool. Remember to just talk about your spouse to a minimum. It is true when it comes to speaking in front of your children or other people that also hang out with your soon-to-be-ex. It may open up a door to the things you are saying, getting back to the narcissist. From there, they will do everything they can to use your words against you.

The narcissist will likely try and use their children as pawns. They will try and gain the upper hand in all things through them. It is likely they will even try to turn their children against the other parent. Please do not participate in the same behaviors, and your children will quickly see that you are a trustworthy parent and genuinely care about them. They will also eventually see that the narcissistic parent is merely trying to manipulate them. It can be a hard situation to face, and you must, above everything else, stay patient and resist the urge to badmouth the narcissist.

No matter how ready you are, there is likely going to be damaged and fallout. It is true of regular divorces, so it is even more real when dealing with a narcissist divorce.

You will be facing high levels of stress, and it will be a test of your endurance. When children are added to this mix, it only makes it more challenging. Know that it is not impossible; you need to be prepared. Take the time to prepare truly. Take notes of what has transpired throughout your relationship and be prepared to talk about all of the horrible things that have occurred. Note the help of your friends and family so that you have the emotional support that you need.

# TIPS ON WHEN YOU PERCEIVE THE PROBLEM AND WHEN YOUR CHILD DOES

**M**any parental separations occur when children are small and unable to understand and comprehend what is happening emotionally. It can be a scary experience for your children who are just learning to express their feelings. There are helpful ways to communicate simply so that your children will understand:

Explain the separation in easy-to-understand terms: "mommy and daddy need to live apart for a while" or "mommy/daddy will be moving away for a bit." If they ask why to explain in simple terms: "sometimes we fight, and we need to spend time away so that we can get along better" or "we need to live separately to be a better mom and dad to you."

Let children know that the decision to separate, and divorce, is about the parents and has nothing to do with them. Make it explicitly clear that they have no fault or reason for the split. One of the separations of the most painful effects has on children is when they fear they are the reason for their parents. A narcissistic parent will make them feel this way at some point, either by blaming the child and the other parent. Keep explaining that they are not to blame and make a point of reminding them as often as needed.

Provide space for your children and allow them to express themselves. It is essential that they feel safe in venting or showing their emotions, as holding it in will only cause them more grief later. If they feel angry and vocalize this to you, validate it for them. Let them know that they have a right to feel this and other emotions.

There is an instinct as a parent that wanted to protect our kids from harm, including emotional hurt and abuse. When a parent reveals their true narcissistic form, it can be difficult to shield children from them, even following a divorce where they are expected to visit the other parent or live with them as part of a custody agreement. When your children are in your care, exercise as much care and kindness as possible. Show your unwavering support for them in all they do and make sure they feel comfortable talking to you. They may want to express frustration about the other parent and explain the hurt they feel, though maybe resisting because they fear you may tell the other parent, or their statements may reach them somehow. For this reason, reassure the kids that anything they divulge is safe with you and that they have no reason to fear any backlash or retaliation at the hands of the other parent. While it may seem easy to convince them, children worry when they don't understand how a process works.

What happens once the separation becomes permanent, and the divorce proceedings begin? Children will need more of an explanation at this point, including what to expect next. Even when kids understand what is going on, they may not comprehend life outside of what they are used to if they (and you) viewed the separation as a temporary circumstance. A simple explanation could suffice; however, more information is needed when there will be a significant change in the way the kids attend school, live, and interact with family and friends. It's important to "fast-forward" to possible results of the divorce so that they know what to expect and to prepare for it:

Where are we going to live? In the early part of the separation, temporary arrangements are made. Usually, one parent will leave the household and live separately for a period, during which both will decide if there is a chance of reconciliation. While the family home remains occupied, change is minimal, and no major upheaval is needed, such as a change in school or living arrangements. The parent who lives apart may agree to pick up the child(ren) according to a temporary arrangement or find a way to meet with the other parent for access and visitation provisions.

What if one of the parents is abusive? In severe cases, the parent leaving maybe you, if you've encountered abuse at the hands of your spouse or have reason to believe they are abusing the children. This can lead to a quick decision, such as seeking refuge with family or friends, or living in a temporary shelter or living situation, until permanent housing can be found. Children may already understand what is happening, though it can be a frightening experience, especially when they are not in a stable home and may have to move more than once following the split. During this time, it's important to stress to your children that the reason for the separation is their safety and well-being. Make it clear that their safety and health are a priority, above all others. It is also essential to impress upon them that moving is temporary and that soon, they will have a new home and feel better again. Keep hope and positivity alive as much as possible, even when you don't feel it yourself. Let the kids know that it is not easy for you and them, but everything will get better in the end by working together.

Staying in contact with friends, family, and arrangements where a transfer in school is necessary. This can be a difficult realization for your child(ren), as they will lose contact with friends at school and family and friends who live nearby. When you have to move, it's important to make arrangements in advance to stay in touch with the people they love, even if it's through online social media and arranging visits now and again. Make a point of calling them regularly and video-calling in real-time to keep your kids connected to the people they will miss once they move. This is an invaluable way for your child(ren) to see that you care about their connections with family and friends by keeping the connection open and continuous. This will also help them understand the importance of bonding and caring for others, which is not something their narcissistic parent will teach them.

It is essential to understand that while every child and situation is unique, most children will need comfort and understanding to feel valued and wanted. This is especially a must when the other parent is a narcissist and tries to manipulate the children into a state of codependence. They will attempt to make the child(ren) feel incapable of doing anything on their own, and that they must rely on the opinion and direction of the toxic parent for all their decisions. This can be done in subtle, minor ways, by criticizing or making them feel incompetent or their opinions unworthy. Comments like "don't be silly/stupid," "you won't make it on your own," and "you are not capable" are just examples of how a toxic parent can make your child's life miserable and cause them to hurt. It will significantly impact their confidence and ability to feel capable of accomplishing goals on their own. There are ways to build a protective barrier with your child to help them cope with a narcissistic parent. The following examples are ways in which you can foster a strong bond with your child(ren) while combatting the negative behavior of your ex and its effect on them:

- Praise them for hard work and encourage them to work towards their goals. When they fail or fall short of their achievements, reassure them of their capabilities and give them as much time and effort as possible to accomplish them. Even where they need assistance, assure them that they can do it on their own.

- Show empathy and explain it to them. Demonstrate the importance of caring for others by inviting them to volunteer and listen to other people's thoughts and feelings. Prioritize to help them understand the value of feeling empathy for other people and how to gauge their responses when handling delicate situations. A narcissist parent will not provide any guidance on empathy, as they are incapable of it.

- One meaningful gift you can provide to your children is unconditional love. This is defined as a love that prevails above all else, regardless of your child's decisions and how they live. It is not an easy road for some parents who co-parent with narcissist ex-spouses, as some children will grow to exhibit signs of narcissism of their own. This can lead to another level of difficulty and conflict. Despite this, you can continue to demonstrate love, even if you don't agree with your children's behavior or how they handle situations. You can constantly reassure them that you love and support them while explaining disapproval of some of their actions. It can be a challenging yet rewarding way to communicate with your children in the long term, as they will always know that you are there for them.

- Change is inevitable during a divorce or separation; whether it involves major overhauls or smaller changes, it's going to impact your children in many ways. Being a supportive, stable parent will help them anchor their lives throughout childhood and as they progress into adulthood. While the ex-spouse connection will be volatile, it's going to be easier for them to cope with you by their side.

# HOW TO HANDLE YOUR EX WHEN HE DENIES YOU ACCESS, INSULTS YOU IN FRONT OF YOUR CHILDREN, OR DOES ANY FAMILY WRONG. TIPS ON HOW TO DEAL WITH AN EX WHO SIMPLY DOESN'T PLAY BY THE RULES

There are several reasons why victims might want to maintain a Low-Contact relationship with a narcissistic abuser. However, suppose a relationship with a narcissist makes you feel that your health, sanity, or safety are under threat. In that case, there is usually only one sensible path to take moving forward, which is to cut them off entirely.

You must set boundaries for yourself and hold yourself accountable for enforcing consequences when a narcissist refuses to recognize or respect them. Never get into the practice of making hollow threats; if you tell a narcissist that your departure is a possible repercussion of a certain behavior, then you must be prepared to leave when they try to test your resolve.

You cannot force a narcissist to respect your boundaries or treat you the way you deserve to be appreciated. Therefore, you are responsible for respecting your boundaries, setting an example for others, and treating yourself well. If nothing but abuse is being served, your best option is to leave the table and show the abuser that you can cook up something far better for yourself.

## Going No-Contact

Going No-Contact is not a tactic, strategy, or mind game, though a narcissist may retaliate by accusing you of harboring these intentions when you employ it. The end goal is not to encourage the narcissist to turn around and chase after you. The end goal is to prevent any further opportunities for abuse, period. Once and for all. When you decide to go No-Contact, you must embrace the notion that this is a non-negotiable state, with no grey area and no more second chances.

That being said, you mustn't expect it to be easy, nor beat yourself up if you find it difficult to maintain zero contact with someone you love, admire, or rely upon. This is challenging for most victims; you would not be the only one to go back on the decision. Experts estimate that victims of narcissistic abuse usually rack up several failed attempts at establishing a boundary of No-Contact before they can successfully maintain it. Seven failed attempts are average; for some people, the cycle lasts much, much longer.

You may feel the urge to announce your decision to the narcissist or ask them to respect your wishes and stop contacting you. This is understandable, but unfortunately, not likely to work as intended. Narcissists often see all forms of contact as a foot-in-the-door; they may interpret your declaration as a thinly veiled invitation to pursue you further or make an over-the-top gesture to get back in your good graces. By contrast, the most effective way to go No-Contact is to disappear and stay gone. Block the narcissist's phone number and email address; stop following them on social media; uninvite yourself from gatherings or institutions where you might run into them by chance. Take power into your own hands, and don't give the narcissist any opportunity to try and steal it back from you.

Remind yourself that you have reached this point because you've already given the narcissist far more than enough chances. Ask yourself: "Is there really anything this person could do to convince me that they've changed, and this won't happen again?" The answer, most likely, is no. You don't owe the narcissist another chance or an explanation. You owe it to yourself to be set free.

## Protecting Yourself and Maintaining Resolve

Set yourself up for success by informing your support system first--ideally shortly before or after cutting the narcissist off. Choose people that you feel are trustworthy, meaning no potential members of the narcissist's harem. It's important to be brutally honest with yourself about the characters and values of the people in your life when you do this; if they are susceptible to seduction by the narcissist, eager to advance in the same career field, envious of the narcissist's trophies and wealth, or just similarly shallow in value structure, they may be better suited to the harem than to your support system, and they'll be reluctant to see what you are trying to show them. The people you choose to share this with will not only be able to hold you accountable to your declaration; they also may be called upon to protect you from the narcissist's future attempts to discredit, devalue, or hoover you back in. Choose them wisely.

Next, get to a few mutual acquaintances you know will be curious about the split. It's best to get to them before the narcissist has a chance to spin their side of the story, but you also want to appear calm and unhurried, so don't trouble yourself to rush this step. What you should tell these people is a detail-free, bare-bones version of the story--no blaming either party or requesting pity, just a statement that things didn't work out. Afterward, you'll go on to explain that you've decided not to be in contact with the narcissist (whom you should reference by their name, not the term "narcissist") anymore and that you'd appreciate their support of your decision. You can even further clarify that they can show this support by not passing messages between either of you, not putting you in a room together without warning, not trying to encourage reconciliation, and so on.

This may certainly arouse their curiosity, but no further divulgement of information is needed for them to respect your stated boundaries. If any of these people are unable to respect these reasonable requests, you have discovered in them a flying monkey who cannot be trusted. Let them go, along with the narcissist; these people were never really on your side.

# How to Handle Smear Campaigns

When a narcissist tries to retaliate by spreading lies about you, their ultimate goal isn't just to change other people's opinions of you; they are also aiming to throw you off-balance.

As difficult as it may be to embrace this reality during a vicious attack on your character, the best way to respond to a smear campaign is not to respond at all. Narcissists are masters at this game, and you probably are not their first target; they may have set things up purposefully in such a way that any reasonable emotional reaction from you will only serve to prove their point. Furthermore, people tend to disbelieve victims who are frantic, furious, or panicked, thinking that those who make a spectacle of themselves are much more likely to be liars than those who appear calm (and the narcissist will appear quite calm, in comparison to your reaction).

Do not engage in arguments with flying monkeys or harem members. Recognize that anyone who buys into the smear campaign is a lost cause and can never be fully persuaded to be on your side or believe you. You're probably better off without them. It might feel shameful to walk away from this situation without trying to stand up for yourself but try to have faith that the truth will prevail if you leave it alone. The more you engage, the more energy you are giving to the narcissist. Instead, use that energy to build new and better relationships or invest in your self-care routine.

# How to Respond to Harassment

While it's best to ignore smear campaigns, forms of harassment that pose a viable threat to your safety are another story altogether. Timestamps, photographs, and messages sent to members of your support system may come in very handy if you decide to bring file a legal complaint. Don't try to be a hero and impress other people with your independence and self-sufficiency; you need witnesses and support.

Though it may be tempting to retaliate, seek vengeance, or try to scare them off, do everything in your power to resist this urge. Narcissistic abusers are extremely likely to flip the script and accuse you of abuse, pressing charges against you even if your reaction is minor compared to their behavior. Understand that their harassment is a baited trap set just for you. The awful thing you can do is walk right into it.

If you cannot involve law enforcement, for whatever reason, realize that there are other ways to back yourself up with institutional power. Allow your family and friends to know that they should never reveal your location or details of your personal life to this abuser and agree upon a code word to use with them if the situation ever becomes dangerous and you need immediate assistance. If possible, try not to get too emotional or cry when making your case to outside parties. As unfair as it may seem, people in your workplace may not take your claims seriously if the report appears dramatic or if you seem wishy-washy about the state of this relationship. Make it clear that you want to prevent this person from ever interfering with your work again and that you would like to have their support in maintaining your privacy. If your dedication to the job is made plain, there is a better chance that you'll be able to get the support and protection you need in that environment.

If you feel that your safety is being threatened or stalking and harassment behaviors have continued to escalate despite your best efforts to deter them, please consider contacting the police and pressing charges. It may help to remind yourself that you are not the only person in danger here; the narcissist is liable to attack other people who interfere in their quest to reach you. Call for law enforcement is the best way to keep yourself and your loved ones protected.

# WAYS TO BUILD RESILIENCE IN CHILDREN WHEN CO-PARENTING WITH A NARCISSISTIC EX

C o-parenting with a narcissist can be an especially difficult endeavor but knowing how to build resilience in children is essential if they're going to survive and thrive while still maintaining their sanity.

Children and narcissists are often thought of as "soul mates" or, at the very least, their mirror image. They have all of the same characteristics, and in many cases, those who've co-parented with a narcissist have found themselves constantly identifying with them. Naturally, survival instincts kick in, which leads them to want to "fix" the narcissist before they can do any further damage to their children.

Unfortunately, this dynamic is often an ill-conceived one. While you may feel that you can't survive without the narcissist in your life, it's important to remember that if you do choose to stay with them, the children are going to be expected to endure as well.

## Children Build Resilience by Finding Their Way

Resilience comes from within and is based on a child's will. There are no shortcuts, only a willingness to recognize the truth and to pursue that truth with all of their heart.

Once you've recognized the truth, you must begin by gaining knowledge about narcissism and narcissistic abuse. You can't fix someone else unless you understand how they think and why they behave the way they do.

Many people who've co-parented with a narcissist have been able to let go of their desire to fix their ex once they truly understand how deeply hurtful and malicious, they can be. They've also learned that they can never control anyone else.

The Golden Rule applies especially well to narcissists because they always do unto others as they would have done unto them. You must realize that what you're about to endure is coming directly from the narcissist's heart. You must expect the unexpected and then let it go. Otherwise, you will find yourself engorging yourself with hate and shame.

Those who have managed to survive (and even thrive) after co-parenting with a narcissist are those who've learned to forgive themselves for not being able to change them while also forgiving them for having done what they've done.

You can never completely rid yourself of pain or the desire to seek revenge, but you can learn to get a clean break from the narcissist and do what's best for your children.

## Children Build Resilience by Internalizing and then Releasing Their Power

There is no particular thing as achieving perfection, only a willingness to evolve and adapt constantly. Don't be afraid to change your mind.

Don't let the narcissist have power over you anymore by giving them ground or giving into them through self-criticism. As they say, "Confidence is never a substitute for competence." Empower yourself by trusting your instincts and being persistent. If you don't succeed at first, keep trying until you figure it out. Build resilience by using adversity as fuel for change and growth.

When narcissists feel threatened or "outraged," they can become incredibly vicious and vitriolic. Don't let them steal your joy.

## Children Build Resilience by Forgiving Others (And Their Parents) While Also Forgiving Themselves

Children who've survived while co-parenting with a narcissist are those who've allowed themselves to be loved even when it didn't make sense to them, and they know what love is now. They've learned to rely on their gut and make decisions based on what truly matters to them. They know how to be present with their feelings, and they know that their growth is far more important than any conflict derived from a narcissist's actions. While it's unlikely that you'll ever achieve true peace with a narcissist, knowing how to build resilience in children will help them cope better, even if they've never come face-to-face with one themselves.

## The Only Thing a Narcissist Fear Is a Child Who Has Built a Resilient Foundation

Easing your son or daughter into the process with physical coping strategies like drawing, coloring, or reading can be a good start.

Resilience building may seem overwhelming and even impossible but remember that you're not alone. You have many resources at your disposal.

The National Domestic Violence Hotline welcomes calls from anyone in an abusive relationship and provides a plethora of resources for those in need.

You can also reach out to the narcissist's family members if you think they might be willing and able to help you.

While it's impossible to change anyone else, you can change your perspective on their behavior by learning how to build resilience in children. Remember that you don't have to feel powerless or hopeless.

# HOW TO SOLVE REAL PROBLEMS AND COMMUNICATION TRICKS FOR DEALING WITH AN EX WHO ACTIVELY UNDERMINES YOUR ROUTINE, DISCIPLINE, VALUES, OR DOMESTIC TRANQUILITY

We will explore how to manage an ex that still shows up in your life. How do you get through to them and communicate with them? How do you deal with a divorce or separation going on that has the potential to ruin your routine, values, and domestic tranquility? In addition, we will also learn some communication tips for dealing with difficult people.

The struggle is real for most of us in love relationships. The pain of separation and the confusion of pursuing or even maintaining the relationship is complicated by stress, drama, and relational baggage. Stress levels can rise above normal levels due to uncertainty, anxiety, over-thinking, etc.

It is challenging to remain calm and focused when dealing with the stress of the breakup. This is because of the intense emotions involved in a divorce, separation, or ending a long-term relationship. Of course, this creates additional stress and confusion in dealing with how to cope with your ex. These exes are often very close to you emotionally yet can also be very confused about the situation. Often, they don't know what they want now or what they want at all.

Most people don't like the idea of being told what to do, but if enough communication can be established with the ex, you can find a path forward. Using communication is very important to feel confident and maintain your sanity. Many tools can be used to communicate well with an ex.

Dealing with an ex, especially when they are contacting you or contacting you a lot, can be very difficult in these challenging times. Managing the process can be extremely hard if both parties don't have the money for lawyers or amicable resolutions. It is possible to solve the most complex issues and personal cases without raising your family in arms.

# Communication Tools

Consider what you want to communicate with your ex. Are you trying to get basic information, make plans, or find out more about the reasoning behind the breakup? Communication tips are very important to determine what you need from them and formulate a plan to meet your needs.

Consider writing or sending an email. However, do you want to have a conversation with your ex? Consider the time of day because some people cannot have phone conversations due to work, family issues, etc. Therefore, texting or emailing is better to start.

In addition, you can consider writing a letter by hand. This can be extremely personal and private, but keep in mind that it isn't secure like a digital message is. Think about how you feel and what you want to say. Don't send it via email or text messaging because others could see it or could be forwarded to the other party without your permission.

The question of if it is better to meet your ex for lunch or just text or call is a very common one. This question can be confusing because many people do not know the best way to communicate with an ex, so they err on the side of caution and want to stay away from their ex. However, other relationships require frequent interaction, and this may not be possible in cases like this. If you're going to see your ex and to talk, then meet them for lunch. If you don't want to meet them, then just text or call.

Some basic rules will help you communicate effectively with an ex and avoid conflict and confrontation. These rules are very simple but effective in dealing with difficult exes: Don't always accept their calls or messages right away. It is best to let them know that you will send them an email or message. This will save you both times, and it will give them a hint that you don't need to deal with the situation.

Don't let them ruin your life. Tell them to back off and leave you alone unless there is an emergency or problem. This is what they want but being responsive to their concerns can lead to a big problem.

Be patient and collected because communication can be difficult when dealing with an ex. Always use good manners and think about what you are going to say before responding. Never let your frustrations defeat you. This will only derail your communication and lead to significant conflict that can spoil your ex's visit or interaction with you.

Always be very polite in your communication. Even though you are angry, try to write your message or email in a very friendly tone. This will allow the other party to know that you care enough about them to communicate correctly and effectively.

After you have decided that divorce is the best option for you, it is time to move forward and start planning for the future. The process of getting a divorce, drafting a separation agreement, and deciding on how to manage the finances are all critical issues that need to be settled quickly.

In this situation, you have to keep your emotions in check because you don't want to make any hasty decisions or cause any financial harm. Making sure you think through every aspect of your upcoming divorce is crucial to move forward with your life. Consider the future you want to live in now. Do you want to be a single parent, or would you prefer to share custody with your ex? This is an important aspect of the divorce and needs to be planned out before discussing it with your ex. The reason for this is apparent; everyone's life changes after divorce. Therefore, the details of your life will change, and disagreements could occur if these details are not worked out first.

In addition, make sure that you are open-minded when it comes to parenting decisions. Consider if the kids would benefit from joint custody or even a shared custody arrangement. Both of these arrangements have pros and cons and will affect everyone involved. However, taking time to think through all of the potential options is essential. Additionally, it is not always easy to know what your ex will agree with, so be sure that you work together towards a mutually agreeable resolution. If you decide to go back to court, consider this process as well, as there are different laws concerning child support and other financial arrangements.

Divorce is also about dealing with the financial aspects of your separation. The first step is to get an attorney that can help you with this process. Make sure that you and your attorney come up with a strategy for both getting through this part of the process and possible objections. This will give you the best chance at getting what you are seeking from the divorce settlement.

If you find it challenging to communicate with your ex, consider hiring a mediator or third-party consultant who can talk with both parties without conflict. This will allow for the conversation to be productive and not hurtful. A mediator will speak directly with your ex and help maintain a healthy and productive dialogue.

# WHAT TO DO WHEN YOUR EX-SPOUSE TRIES TO TURN THE KIDS AGAINST YOU

**T**here has been a great debate over the claim that parental alienation is a phenomenon that rises to the level of a psycho-emotional syndrome. The parent is then perceived to have malicious intent or serious psycho-emotional pathology.

In parental alienation, one parent works out of neediness or rage to prevent the kids from having a fine relationship with the other parent.

However, as in all human conflict, it takes two to tango.

Is the parent suffering at the hands of the alienating parent equally responsible for their predicament? No.

Are they unconsciously contributing to the problem and playing into the toxic parent's hands? Likely, yes.

## The Court Provides a Framework

Take note that the family court does not have a case management function. That is, once you are done with your basic order, you are expected to make it work—despite the complications of family schedules and parenting children in general. At best, the court can only provide the parents with a framework or foundation to construct their ongoing co-parenting relationship. It's up to the parents to fill in the numerous blanks that occur in raising kids.

This means the court does not monitor or amend the custody orders as situations on the ground change from day to day. Judges deal with discrete issues that are brought before them. These include:

- Formal filing of a motion to create a custody label (legal and physical custody)
- Custody timeshare orders (percentage of time in each parent's care)
- Modifying existing orders

If a parent fails to live up to the letter or intent of the orders, returning to court via the filing of a new motion is your ultimate recourse.

# What Parental Alienation Looks Like

Here's a rough sketch of how parental alienation plays out. A needy, envious, or angry parent creates a "special" bond with the children. This is usually characterized by a peer-type relationship with the kids.

The alienating parent creates a dynamic in which the kids become overly dependent on the parent by treating them as if they are still babies that need care only this parent can provide. At the same time, they treat the kids as peers making them feel entitled to do whatever they want, especially at the other parent's home.

A child will then want to be in the care of the "nurturing" (alienating) parent while simultaneously talking to their other parent as if they were equals.

When the disrespected parent responds with anger or discipline, the children run to the alienating parent, claiming to be treated harshly. The targeted parent feels they are being perceived and treated by the kids the same way by the alienating parent. It's true. The kids will indeed disrespect and devalue the parent in the identical way the alienating parent does.

In a healthy post-separation dynamic, a parent presented with reports of harsh treatment by the kids will communicate with their co-parent, then, if appropriate, support the co-parent's response to the acting out behaviors, not so in the case of the alienating parent. They will concur with the kids that the other parent is mean and doesn't understand them. They are allowed, even encouraged, to stand up to the other parent as their equal. Compounding this situation, the alienating parent has shown the kids that their undivided loyalty is required to maintain their "special" relationship. This is communicated by subtle nonverbal cues that the kids recognize. They are not told in so many words. The children know it by seeing how the parent responds to anyone that the parent dislikes.

# Understanding the Hidden Emotions

What's going on emotionally for the kids is not as it appears on the surface. Despite their cruel, disrespectful attitude toward the alienated parent, feeling compelled to choose between their parents causes them a tremendous amount of stress. Children's identities and sense of self-esteem come from their attachment to both parents. The kids' hurtful behavior masks many conflicted emotions, including anger at having been put in the loyalty bind by the alienating parent.

The healthy parent needs to realize the kids are compelled to behave inappropriately toward them to avoid rejection by the alienating parent. The solution to this is twofold. First, realize that any emotional reactivity will trigger more resistance from the kids regardless of how justified it is.

Responding to the kids or the alienating parent harshly out of anger and exasperation will be used to show what a horrible parent you are. It will prove to an objective observer that all the flaws the alienating parent has accused you of are true. Again, we see that acting out of righteous indignation and anger not only doesn't get us the resolution we want, but it also makes matters much worse.

Often, this is when the alienating parent files a motion to gain sole custody of the kids. The alienating parent will have created a situation where the kids tell the court they no longer want to be with the healthy parent because that parent is mean to them. And from the kids' perspective, this is an accurate depiction.

In this dynamic, the children are not deliberately behaving inappropriately but rather doing what they instinctively know is necessary to keep the alienating parent's "love." So, when the victimized parent reacts angrily, all the kids see is anger and not the rationale behind it.

## Measure Your Responses and Focus on the Kids

Once again, the solution is to change your mind. Think before you respond. Imagine a judge or family court services mediator reading every email and text that you send. More critically, shift your focus away from the toxic parent and back to maintaining the best possible relationship with your kids. This may require you to pick your battles with the kids more carefully. Don't impose punishment that's going to push them away. An authoritarian approach will play into the alienating parent's hand.

Does this mean that you adopt the same approach as the toxic parent and let the kids get away with behaving poorly? No, but if you focus on changing your kids' behavior through discipline, you risk driving a wedge into your relationship. It's healthier for your connection with the kids to let an occasional infraction slide.

This is what it means by it takes two to tango. You can choose to defuse the clashes with the children or become so rigid in your responses that you unwittingly contribute to the toxic parent's plan. I've seen parents become so exasperated that the children end up having no privileges, including cell phones and other electronics. Unfortunately, the children end up hating and disconnecting from the healthy parent.

## Neutral, Therapeutic Support

The second part of the solution is to enlist clinical support. Without the input of a neutral third party, the dynamic can never rise above the level of "he said, she said," in the opinion of the family court. Therapeutic intervention allows each parent to remove the kids from the center of this destructive co-parenting pattern.

A typical clinical program would involve therapy for the children and adjunct family therapy to facilitate communication between the kids and the alienated parent. This intervention is helpful to the kids and gives the alienated parent some support for those relationships. Also, if requested, the clinical specialist can provide objective input about the family dynamic to the family law court.

As a rule, the alienating parent will pay lip service to the idea of therapeutic intervention, then proceed to sabotage all efforts to implement it. The alienating parent's strength is in seducing the kids to take their side in an attempt to manipulate the court system. This correctly implies that the alienating parent has encouraged the kids to become directly involved in custody. Remember, this kind of parentification of the kids is often a key characteristic of alienation.

The alienating parent will share the details of the case as if the kids are peers rather than children that need protection from conflict. They also encourage the kids to confront the other parent on issues that the alienating parent wishes to dominate. For example, the alienating parent may deliberately sign the kids up for extracurricular activities that occur during the other parent's custody time without getting advance consent as required by joint legal custody requirements.

If the healthy parent objects to this intrusion, the kids become furious at that parent's lack of support for their interests. The parent is put into a no-win situation. The kids are effectively put in control through the alienating parent's behavior, and any attempt to set appropriate, healthy limits results in an angry backlash. This type of scenario can lead to the kids stating their preference to live with the alienating parent.

The ability to change your mind and focus on your relationship with the kids rather than reacting to the other parent's provocation is crucial. The biggest challenge is tempering their reaction to the feelings of loss, helplessness, and exasperation that naturally come from being run over by a self-centered or narcissistic personality.

The relentless focus on the healthy parent's / toxic parent creates the perception that they are unwilling to look at their contribution to the process. It's also a waste of energy as you will certainly not be able, nor will the family court endeavor to, change the alienating parent in any fundamental way. You can only hope to create a strong bond with your children that will withstand the constant barrage of intrusion and undermining by the alienating parent and enlist the support of professionals and the court.

# PARENTAL ALIENATION SYNDROME

This is a deep and often misunderstood phenomenon that occurs when one parent purposely manipulates, threatens, punishes, or brainwashes the child into showing and feeling anger, hatred, or resentment toward the other parent. It can destroy a family by hurting children and creating emotional instability. Parental Alienation Syndrome (PAS) is not simply a parental disagreement with each other on how to raise a child. Nor is it evidence of normal arguing between parents who have split up.

PAS occurs when one parent uses manipulation and brainwashing techniques to get a child to reject the other parent with bad feelings. A parent having difficulty adjusting to their separation or divorce may be vulnerable to creating a Parental Alienation Syndrome situation.

The problem with Parent Alienation Syndrome is that it poisons tender emotions, leading to confusion and serious emotional problems.

When a child feels responsible for their parents' separation, it leaves the child feeling guilty and shameful. The vindictive parent then exploits this guilt and shame to turn the child against the other parent.

People who want to help must realize that the PAS situation is a cyclical pattern of behavior with no apparent end.

PAS creates stress internalized by the children, or it may manifest itself in aggressive acting out behaviors. This type of emotional and physical stress can lead to a wide range of symptoms, including irrational fears, depression, anxiety, panic disorder, and dyslexia. These situations are immensely difficult for children as well as adults.

In the United States, several lawsuits against alleged PAS have been filed over the last few years. Some have resulted in settlements of over $100 million. Other cases are working their way through the court system.

One case involved a custodial father who temporarily took his son away from his estranged wife while he and the boy were on a vacation trip. When he brought his son back, it was evident to everyone concerned that something had changed dramatically in the child's attitude toward the mother and her new husband. The boy began to refuse visitation with his mother and her husband, started getting bad grades in school, became violent, and began using drugs.

The child's behavior was explained as being due to the problems of the custodial father. A custody evaluation was ordered, and a therapist recommended that the child should live with his mother.

No one found out that the child had been warned that living with his father would result in physical punishment from his stepfather. This warning was given in the presence of a social worker.

The custody order was appealed, and a federal court-appointed guardian ad litem supervise the case. The judge requested that both parents be brought before the court. When they arrived in court, the child began screaming at his mother and throwing things at her. The judge then ordered that the child not see his mother again until he could behave properly in the court.

The child's mother then contacted a lawyer who filed a lengthy appeal alleging that the child's problems were due to custody. The appeals court agreed and ordered that the boy lives with his mother until he was fourteen. When he was fourteen, the judge finally decided that the boy should choose which parent he would live with. This means that both parents will have very little control over his life from now on.

The point of this is to show how a Parental Alienation Syndrome situation will not go away, and in fact, gets worse. The child's current problems directly result from a separation that did not have any real basis.

The boy's stepfather was clearly at fault for creating the PAS situation in the child. However, you could also blame the judge who failed to see what was happening and who ordered a custody evaluation before it was warranted.

The problem is that the judge did not see the whole picture in its entirety. Both parents were emotionally blind to what was happening to their son. One parent had a mental problem, and the other didn't recognize it. In addition, both parents were blind to their weaknesses.

If you look at this situation, you will see that it could have been avoided if one or more people (or parties) involved would have recognized the problem and taken action before it got any worse.

Figure out what brought about this problem. Then we need to look at the people involved, including ourselves, and see if there are any other situations like this anywhere else in our lives.

In most cases, when you follow the money trail, you will find that PAS cases are caused by someone who wants to use children for some purpose that has nothing to do with their welfare. In other words, someone wants something and will go to almost any length to get it.

Because of this exploitation, the emotional problems created by PAS can be devastating for the child. The child's self-worth is diminished, and he feels sad and angry. He hates himself for being manipulated and brainwashed into believing that his mother or the other parent is the one to blame for everything wrong in his life.

# ADVICE FOR EACH AGE OF YOUR CHILD

**P**arenting one size doesn't fit all. The same is valid for talking with your children about the divorce. Every child is at a different developmental stage that requires you to adapt what you say to meet individual levels of maturity and understanding. In every developmental stage, these constants apply:

- Shield children from parental hostility and conflict.
- Give frequent reassurances of your love.
- Create and follow a predictable parenting plan.
- Remain engaged in parenting.

## Older Toddlers: 18 Months to 3 Years

If you have a toddler, you are undoubtedly quite familiar with their strong need to be independent. They test limits and begin to express opinions. A primary developmental task for toddlers is to learn to be unique and separate individuals. Temper tantrums and loudly expressed "No!" From a developmental standpoint, a lot is going on at this stage. It is difficult for parents to recognize whether the uproar is related to the divorce or is developmentally normal. Signs of distress may include acting sad or lonely, changes in eating or sleeping habits, fears of once-familiar activities or things, and regression to behaviors from an earlier stage of development such as thumb sucking, baby talk, fear of sleeping alone, asking for a bottle, or wanting to wear a diaper again.

As with infants, providing a consistent, predictable routine where their needs are met will help your toddler adjust to the many changes divorce brings. Your toddler will need frequent reassurance of your love through your actions as well as your words. A parenting schedule where they regularly spend time with each of you is optimal. Toddlers do best to go no more than three to five days without seeing one parent.

### What to Do

Since toddlers don't have a good concept of time, helping them know when they will be at each house will ease transition jitters. Make a calendar where they can see it and use stickers or colored pens to designate "Mom time" and "Dad time." Help them count the number of nights of sleep. For example, "You have three nights of sleep with Mommy, and then you go to Dad's house. Let's count them together, one, two, and three, Daddy." The more light-hearted and matter of fact your tone, the better for your toddler.

Children love books about themselves. Make a small book with photographs of familiar items and routines at each parent's house and read it together before changing homes. I've known children to carry these books until the paper is nearly worn through. Check your library or bookstore for age-appropriate books about divorce.

### What to Say

Toddlers need a short and simple explanation about the divorce. You will have to repeat it many times as they work to understand what it means.

# Preschoolers: 3 to 5 Years

Preschoolers experience a huge boost in cognitive and physical abilities. They are more self-sufficient than before and can carry out basic self-care tasks. Their vocabulary has increased, allowing them to understand better and express feelings and ideas. Preschoolers can be big talkers! Even with this growth in cognitive ability, there are still areas of confusion. For example, if they overhear parents discussing or arguing about parenting time, they are very likely to make an inaccurate conclusion that they are responsible for the divorce.

Preschoolers benefit from routine and a predictable schedule. They can feel overwhelmed by the multiple changes that accompany divorce. They are sometimes afraid a parent will abandon them.

Preschoolers may show signs of distress like clinginess or fear of exploring the world, regressing to earlier developmental stages, feeling responsible for the divorce or a parent's feelings, acting sad, showing uncharacteristic outbursts of anger, and trying to control their environment.

### What to Do

As you talk with your preschooler about the divorce, assure him of your love and abiding presence in his life. Breathe calmly, smile, and relax as you describe what's going to happen. Gently touch a hand or rub your child's back as you talk.

### What to Say

Reassurance and comfort are the keys to the game with preschoolers. Tell them what's going to happen without turning it into a crisis.

# Early School Agers: 6 to 8 Years

School-age children are becoming quite savvy about the world. Their cognitive abilities are growing by leaps and bounds, giving them a much broader understanding of feelings and the ability to regulate them better. Family relationships are important and provide a strong base from which to venture into the world of school and friends. When the divorce disrupts this secure base, it can affect the normal developmental milestone of moving away from the family as the primary source of social interactions.

Children at this age are well aware of rules and become very disappointed when they believe a parent isn't following rules. They deeply miss the parent they are not with and sometimes side with one parent against the other.

Signs of distress include major changes in grades or attitudes about school, increased physical symptoms like headaches and stomachaches, exaggerated emotions like moping, crying, acting sad or lonely, and a general lack of enthusiasm.

## What to Do

Provide a loving environment for your children. Maintain a predictable routine with clearly communicated expectations for behavior. Be a good listener, accepting all feelings while you help your children attach words to the feelings they share. Keep your children away from any conflict you may have with the other parent. Be that secure base they need as they go out and explore.

## What to Say

At this age, your children will want some details. They've probably noticed the conflict and maybe anticipating your news about the divorce. Even so, they will need a gentle explanation and reassurance of your love.

# Preteens: 9 to 12 Years

In this developmental stage, children become even more independent, and friends play an important role in their lives. Preteens are much more aware of what other people think, especially their peers. They might feel ashamed or embarrassed about the divorce, sometimes to the point of keeping quiet about it. They are selfishly and appropriately focused on their own lives, and they don't like it when they see the divorce messing things up for them.

Preteens have made huge leaps in cognitive ability and are better able to understand the nuances of parents' problems. They are likely to feel torn between parents, and they worry when they believe a parent isn't okay. Conflicts tend to occur when they don't get something they want. They are usually very good at pushing guilt buttons, blaming parents, and the divorce when things don't go as they'd like.

Signs of distress about the divorce show increased physical symptoms like headaches, stomachaches, or general "just not feeling well"; a dramatic change in grades or attitudes about school; fighting with peers or siblings; acting like the divorce is no big deal and premature sexual activity.

### What to Do

Your preteen will vigilantly watch how you handle things and will be reasonably quick to judge your actions. Parents need to model good self-care and healthy ways to express emotions. Preteens need to involve and alert parents to help them with the increasingly complex issues they face in the world. They will want to know what's going on and will push for details. Be cautious about how much you share. They can handle more information than younger children, but they must be protected from the specifics of adult problems.

### What to Say

Your preteens will hold you accountable for your actions, sometimes brutally so. When you talk with them about the divorce, it's essential to keep it real and be honest without sharing too much.

## Adolescents: 13 to 19 Years

The primary developmental task for adolescents is to get ready to leave home and live in the adult world. Yet, they aren't entirely as prepared as they may think. There are developmental milestones to achieve. They have their version of "magical thinking," where they believe bad things could never happen to them. Part of their parent's job is to compassionately help them learn responsibility for their actions as they gain experience to leave the nest successfully.

Like preteens, adolescents are focused on themselves. They resent the divorce when it disrupts their lives. Because of divorce, they may have greater responsibilities at home, less money, and overworked and unavailable parents. Teens' cognitive ability has increased to make them think like adults, although they aren't quite there yet. They are good at figuring out what's going on with their parents and will endlessly push for details. Be cautious about sharing too much because it isn't in their best interest.

Teens that are getting ready to leave home feel anxious about this huge step and will need compassionate parents mentally and physically be available as they work through the fear and excitement. Teens may feel some responsibility for the breakup because of things they did or did not do. It's important to reassure them the divorce in no way is their fault.

Signs of distress include premature sexual activity, excessive drug or alcohol use, problems in the school including truancy or suspension, negative attitude, criticisms of parents, leaving home prematurely, or showing reluctance to leave, canceling college plans, and moving out.

## What to Do

Maintain stability in your teen's living arrangements with a few life changes as possible. Teens need reasonable limits with clearly articulated expectations and consequences. Parents must stay attentive and keep on top of monitoring daily activities. There is a great need for excellent communication between parents around rules, curfews, homework, cell phones, Internet use, and cars.

## What to Say

Teens will be very interested in the logistics of your divorce and will do best when they have a say in the schedule. They want to know you are taking their needs into account. If possible, reassure them that their activities and interactions with friends won't change. They need to be told they aren't responsible for the divorce. Because their social lives are busy, teens do best with plenty of warning before changes occur in the family schedule. Offer multiple times to talk about what will happen and then compassionately answer their questions. The sample script for preteens also works for adolescents.

# POSITIVE PARENTING APPROACH IN DEALING WITH A HOSTILE EX-SPOUSE

Y ou have learned that taking things personally and losing your control feeds into your narcissistic ex's behavior. They will continue to do things to spite you, manipulate you or your children, and always have their own best interests at heart—not your child's. By limiting contact, setting parental guidelines, providing structure for yourself, modeling healthy communication, and ignoring the narcissist's attempts to abuse you, you can focus more on your child. In this co-parenting situation, your child's development is of crucial importance.

## Encourage Individuality

Children are influenced by everything and everyone in their world. A narcissist will make them believe they have to please everyone or "bow down" to their peers to feel loved or appreciated. The child of a narcissist is not an individual but a reflection of them. Being a non-narcissistic parent, you can counteract these habits by helping your child realize that they are their person. As all children like to follow their parent's lead, make sure to model positive mannerisms to help them figure out the difference between 53 impolite behavior and kindness. Seek opportunities for your child to grow independently, such as:

- Providing creative activities
- Asking them which sports or summer camp they would like to join
- Journaling their thoughts and feelings
- Letting them choose their clothes and toys

## Encourage Self-Esteem

Self-esteem is built through unconditional love and acknowledgment. Build positive reinforcement through the milestones your child accomplishes in their lives. Give them praise when it's needed, not when they do something to gain your affection. Narcissists have a high, self-absorbed image, and so their love will only ever be conditional as long as your child serves them and their needs. More ways to counteract this are:

- Tell your child that they are smart or good (when they are good) to remind them that they have good traits.

- Praise them for things like going potty on their own, winning third place at the fair, or displaying good behavior with their friends.
- Be careful with what you say to them, like—"you are so awesome in my eyes" rather than "you are the most awesome person in the whole wide world."

## Help Build Self-Confidence

Your child is always taking in new information and building skills to boost their self-confidence. Reward them by saying things like, "wow, you are good at that; show me again." Or "some things take practice, why don't we try again?" In doing this, you allow your child to figure out their strengths and weaknesses, which encourages independence and teaches them to develop confidence in the things they can do while letting go of perfecting what they can't. Try this:

- Enlist your child up for a sports team.
- Encourage them to try new things.
- Explain that being fearful is their body's way of reacting to change and that change is a good thing.

## Allow Mistakes to Be Opportunities

A narcissistic parent will ensure that their child strives to be the best and only rewards them when they are the best. This promotes perfectionism and results in temper tantrums when your child can't impress. Teach your child:

Mistakes will happen but are needed to grow into happy individuals.

Make a mistake on purpose before your child, and don't make it a big deal. Like paint together and "accidentally" color out of the lines. Say oops and laugh about it.

Challenge them to do things they don't enjoy doing or are not good at, then applaud their efforts and say, "good job for trying."

Do not exaggerate their accomplishments, as focusing too much on this can put pressure on them, encouraging perfectionist behavior.

# Create Positive Influences and Environments for Your Child

Creating a stable environment for your child—one where they will feel safe, secure, and confident—will keep their minds at ease during the switch between parents. As hard as this is for you to co-parent with your ex, it is even harder for your children to adapt to such change. Building a community of support can help aid you in this difficult transition. This can also help your child make positive connections and learn from others—not just you.

# Teaching Your Child Empathy

All children and teens are selfish individuals, which is part of their development to independence and individuality. However, it doesn't become a problem unless there is no remorse or feelings behind their actions. You can teach them empathy by:

- Always remind them that other people have feelings, too.
- When reading or watching TV, ask your child how they think the person feels.
- When your children do something good or bad to someone else, ask them how they would feel if it had been done to them. This will help them realize the other person's feelings.

# Explaining the Importance of Friends and Family

Narcissists are usually lonely and sheltered. They rarely have friends come over, and they rarely let their children have playdates. Children can pick up on these patterns and use their friends in the same way through manipulation or exploitation. To counteract this:

- Inspire your child to make healthy bonding relationships.
- Role model healthy interaction.
- Host a get-together and invite friends for your child while modeling laughter and fun times.
- Demonstrate loyalty, sharing, and effective communication skills.

# Discipline and Explain Manipulation Tactics Used by Your Child

Every child will push limits and boundaries to see what they can and cannot get away with. This is where positive reinforcement and discipline come in. Catch their malicious acts, pull them aside, and explain at eye level how unhealthy this type of communication is. Tell them a better way to handle the situation and ignore or overlook negative tantrums. When you feed into the positive, you develop positive attitudes. When you give attention to the anger and negativity, it allows them to continue because even though throwing hissy fits, they are still getting a reaction out of you.

If your child tries to manipulate their friend by saying, "if you don't do xxx, I won't xxx," catch their behavior and tell them that holding something over someone else's head is inappropriate and will not be tolerated. Let them know that they cannot control someone else, but they can do their own thing if their friend isn't playing nicely.

Role model to them that the kinder you are, the more beneficial rewards you will get. Explain to them that through effective communication and being polite, people will likely want to help you rather than fear you.

Every time they do something positive on their terms later, pull them aside and tell them how proud you are of handling the situation the way they did.

# HOW TO WORK WITH THE THERAPIST

Whenever you are healing from any form of abuse, it is always advised that you work with a therapist who can help you completely recover from the abuse you have faced in your life. Especially in a situation as complex as healing from narcissism, having a therapist can help you work through the challenging emotions and realizations and have compassion for yourself. They can also support you in developing healthier coping methods and self-care routines while keeping you accountable in your commitment to living a healthier life.

It is recommended to combine self-help with professional therapists. Read as much as you can, surround yourself with supportive people, and do everything you can to educate yourself on what you are going through and how you can successfully get through it. Then, consult a professional therapist who can help you in ways that you cannot help yourself, which would not be available through loved ones or books. The therapist will help you understand your unique situation, create custom strategies for healing and coping based on personal needs, and ultimately support you in feeling safe and comfortable during the entire experience.

## Self-Validate Your Right to Seek Help

It is an excellent time for you to practice self-validation as you understand that you have a right to seek help and that you deserve the help you desire. This opportunity can prove your commitment to yourself and your needs, assert boundaries in your mind to the thoughts that tell you that you do not need help, and forgive yourself for your fears around help. You can even use this as a time to label and work through the emotions you are having around the idea of hiring a therapist in the first place to seek help.

# Find a Trauma-Informed Therapist

In finding a therapist, you need to find a trauma-informed therapist. These days, many therapists make an effort to be trauma-informed, which means that there should be no shortage of therapists available to you to help you with what you are going through. With that being said, do make sure that when you are looking for a therapist, you ask them what sorts of trauma they have helped people heal from and their philosophies on healing from trauma. Knowing that your therapist understands your unique type of situation and what you might be going through, can help assure you that they will believe you and be helpful to your healing experience.

# Create a Sense of Safety in Your Client-Therapist Relationship

When you work with a therapist, always make sure that you pick one who helps you feel safe and supported right from day one. It might be challenging to tell if you are particularly afraid of visiting a therapist in general. Still, typically you will know because you will speak with a therapist who seems to help you feel better. You should pick a therapist who helps you feel more comfortable and supported from the start, as this is a therapist that you are likely to develop a good relationship with. If you find a therapist with whom you do not feel comfortable, recognize that this is likely a mismatch between you and your therapist's personality and not evidence that therapy will not help you.

If you are afraid of visiting your therapist, even if you think that fear sounds silly or strange, do not be afraid to open up about this. You could even make this your first area of focus so that you can test the waters to see how your therapist responds to your emotions and your needs. In many instances, sharing this will help you feel more confident and allow your therapist to understand your needs while also showing you that they are there to help you, not judge or hurt you.

Lastly, keep the topic of your therapist away from your partner unless you truly feel the need to tell them. Telling them that you go to therapy, or saying that you go because of them, could expose you to being abused for your choice, which could compromise your willingness to continue going. Keep some things to yourself. You can do so by asserting the boundary that you are not required to tell your mother everything can be incredibly helpful in establishing a sense of security in your client-therapist relationship.

# WAYS TO PROTECT YOUR CHILDREN FROM LOYALTY CONFLICTS

U nfortunately, even with a detailed child arrangement plan in place, there will be times when disagreements and conflicts will be unavoidable. You may have to accept the likelihood of this, as well as the fact that it will largely fall upon you, as the non-narcissistic parent, to shield the children from such conflict as far as you are able.

The narcissist is likely to:

- Treat the children sub-optimally because they know no other way.
- Badmouth and lie about you to them to punish you.
- Use the children as a means through which they can legitimately maintain contact with you and keep some form of control. The children are likely to be your 'Achilles' heel' and, therefore, an excellent button to repeatedly press.
- Use them to cause pain to you with no regard whatsoever to the consequences of the children being caught in the middle.
- Make numerous court threats via the children.

You have a very difficult line to tread—between enabling the narcissist's bad behavior and openly denigrating it. Neither is ideal and in truth, there is no perfect answer to these dilemmas.

## What You Can Do

Try to avoid a 'knee-jerk reaction to the narcissist's behavior in front of the children. Count to ten, go into another room, rant in your journal, or to a friend. Only once you've got things off your chest and returned to a place of rational thinking can you respond logically and calmly.

Pick your battles carefully. Do not give your children a childhood in which the predominant memories are friction and litigation between their parents over them.

Accept that the court system is unlikely to be your salvation. It might be the only option in extreme situations, but in most cases, court action will only fuel narcissistic supply and make matters worse.

Carefully consider whether discussing the narcissist's behavior directly with them will have any positive outcome or whether it will just feed the drama. There are occasions where you may have to accept things as they are. You can only be responsible for your parenting and asking the narcissist to cooperate with you in adopting a certain parenting style is likely to be met with deliberate opposition.

Shield the children from the disputes between the two of you as much as you can by not offloading on them or trying to get them to see your point of view rather than the narcissists. Stick your nose in the air and try to take the moral high ground.

Try as hard as you can not to allow the children to become aware of how annoyed you are by the narcissist's manipulations via them. The effort required to maintain an outward image of calmness may well be Herculean. Again, offload on your friends, not on them.

Expect times when your children will be unfairly turned against you and run with it. If the children are old enough, you can calmly suggest that if they would like to know anything about you, they can ask you directly. An explanation that if a person is angry with another person, they sometimes do not tell nice stories about them may also be helpful to younger children here. It is fine to contradict stories that are being told about you without specifically accusing the narcissist of lying—clarify what is true about you rather than directly labeling the narcissist's lies as lies.

In situations where you can see the narcissist manipulating children against one another, try to provide support and reassurance, but don't involve the narcissist again. This will be exactly what the narcissist wants—to create chaos within the family and, consequently, be firmly placed back in the center.

If you can demonstrate equality between children and show no favoritism, you will be teaching them by example that no one child is better than the other in your household. Again, showing empathy, encouraging them to talk about their feelings, and taking those feelings will benefit here—something that the narcissist will not be able to do. All you can do is lead by example.

If the narcissistic parent refuses to pull their weight as Mum or Dad, for example, not turning up to the school concert, sports day, or parents' evening, try not to leave the children feeling that the other parent doesn't care, but at the same time avoid making excuses for the narcissist.

While you might want to avoid discussing the other parent's behavior with children, even if they are teenagers, you can still discuss with them their reactions and feelings about it. You can treat the situation very 'matter of fact' without using it as an opportunity to highlight to the children how useless the other parent is. A response such as "That's a shame for you—I understand that you are disappointed" doesn't judge the other parent but does acknowledge that the child is allowed to have feelings (something which, of course, the narcissistic parent will be invalidating or ignoring).

When it comes to poor behavior, compensating for it or excusing it is a no-no, and so, of course, is exploiting it and using it to work in your favor. But they were completely ignoring it or pretending that it is okay when the risk is that the children may normalize the behavior. You can act consistently in a way that naturally contrasts your behavior with the poor behavior of the narcissist without specifically talking about it. Be on time, show empathy, encourage the children to develop their interests, celebrate who they are as individuals, support them in their ambitions and dreams, and teach them how to have boundaries. Listen to them, talk to them, and get to know them. Be a grown-up—all things their narcissistic parent patently will not do.

As they grow up, they will form their view and develop their adult relationships with both parents. They may decide not to have any relationship with one or the other parent, but that should be left to their adult judgment.

There is, sadly, an element of crossing your fingers regarding the amount of emotional and developmental damage that will be done to them while not in your care. But remember that even the 'best parents inflict some damage on their children. It is part of everybody's life journey to overcome that damage. This is something you have limited control over—some acceptance and self-compassion may be necessary here.

# HOW TO AVOID PARENTAL ALIENATION SYNDROME

**M**any children in divorce or custody disputes face parental alienation syndrome when one parent or relative actively attempts to damage the relationship between their child and the other parent. This is a potentially life-threatening situation, as it can lead them to be the target of ongoing psychological abuse from that person.

The most common form of parental alienation syndrome is caused by a child's grandparents, as this can range from feelings of rejection and anger to physical violence. The child will generally be upset and frightened at attempting to wreak havoc on the relationship between them and the other parent.

As this usually occurs after a period of alleged negligence on the part of the couple involved, they may decide to take action against them. They will want the court to find that the parents have been mentally unfit to raise their children. Evidence might include statements by the child of being regularly beaten or verbally abused, and these will often be picked up by the courts later.

Parental alienation can be difficult for parents to deal with because it is often very subtle and hard to recognize.

In many cases, children can maintain contact with the other parent while being alienated by the other parent or relative, and they can describe their experiences accurately.

To avoid parental alienation syndrome, parents must remember that it is extremely important to communicate with their children so that they can feel comfortable speaking about any issues that may arise.

The basis of the solution for avoiding parental alienation lies in good communication between the parents.

If a parent does not feel comfortable communicating with the other parent, they should turn to the child and discuss their feelings.

It may be necessary for them to communicate with a third party, such as a therapist. They should be aware that while they may feel that they are not getting their point across, children will eventually see through any attempt to alienate them.

If the parents can work together and keep an open dialogue, they will be less likely to fall victim to parental alienation syndrome.

Parents may need professional help from a therapist if they cannot resolve issues with one another. They should remember that this form of alienation syndrome can worsen if no effective action is taken.

# Techniques for Talking to Your Children in Ways that Foster Honesty and Trust

No matter how small the issue, it doesn't hurt to hold a family discussion at the beginning and end of each day. Just be sure you start with something positive — something such as "I love you, and I'm glad we're together."
Make a list of your favorite features about each child on separate pieces of paper.
Let them pick one thing they can share with their partner — even if it's something so small as loving to eat an ice cream cone.
Periodically, ask each child to talk about what they love most about the other parent.
This is the best way to help them maintain their relationships with each parent separately and your relationship with one another as a family.
Do everything you can to keep your children in contact with the other parent financially and on holidays, even if this is difficult for one or both of you.
One common strategy for resolving conflict in custody battles involves "parenting coordinators" who are trained to offer their services at no cost. They offer to facilitate communication between parents and children and mediate between parents, but custodial parents or their attorneys do not hire them.
These mediators are trained to listen actively to the children. They are required to adopt a non-judgmental attitude that maintains the child's sense of being valued in their own unique identity and life.
If parents have difficulty working out their differences through an informal meeting between themselves and their children, they may find these services helpful. Some believe that the involvement of these services does not make a difference.
In some cases, judges have ordered that these therapists be paid with public funds through the custodial parent. In others, the court has ruled that they are a family matter, and only parties involved can rule what is best for their children.
A further strategy involves a social worker or psychologist who both parents hire.
This person will evaluate all of their interactions with their children and make recommendations on how to resolve conflicts between parents without involving the courts.
For example, such a worker might suggest that one parent set aside a certain time to meet with the other parent in a neutral place.
They may also suggest that the parents take turns speaking alone with their children about their feelings and may offer other suggestions.
Sometimes these workers will offer to mediate between parents to get them to agree on a specific arrangement or schedule for parenting time until they can resolve their conflicts independently. If they cannot get the parents to agree on such an arrangement, the court may appoint a guardian (or assign a mediator) without their consent.

# WHEN YOUR EX IS BRAINWASHING YOUR CHILDREN

The parent that has the least amount of time with the child is always going to struggle with their lack of involvement in the child's day-to-day life. After all, this interaction has been a staple of most parents' commitment to their children and with their families. Keep in mind that your children are also adjusting to this change and may have real issues with the fact that one parent is no longer in their life as much as before. Typically, this is true of children of all ages.

However, older kids often feel a stronger sense of abandonment or loss since they are more aware of the divorce issues.

When both parents work together to understand that divorce is an issue between adults and not between the parent and the children, this anger and anxiety will fade away. Again, both parents have to help the children understand the dynamics of divorce. Facilitate the children understanding that both Mom and Dad are important people in the life of the child or children and that both parents will continue to work together. This is the non-toxic side of divorce that children need to be exposed to.

But when one parent intentionally minimizes or prevents the child from not spending time with the targeted parent, it steps across the line into alienation. Sometimes — although rarely — these controlling parents even go to jail for non-compliance with the court-ordered visitation times. And then they will twist this around to how much they love the child and how worried they are about sending their child into a "harmful" environment. In addition, they aren't above putting the child on a guilt trip about their stint in jail since they constantly talk about how they would do anything to "protect" the child from spending time with the other "unsafe" parent.

Take advantage of all the time granted in your divorce decree. Don't allow long-time gaps between contact. Even if you can't spend physical time together, making phone calls, sending text messages and emails, and cards to the kids is essential. This helps thwart alienation since you continue to be the same caring parent even though you aren't around as much as before.

Unfortunately, alienating parents use this time away from the other parent to systematically coach, manipulate, and reprogram the child's thinking about the other parent. This intentional mind molding occurs over weeks, months, and years.

Child therapists working in Parental Alienation Syndrome and brainwashing indicate that increased, positive contact with the targeted parent is the key to breaking the negative cycle. Even if the alienating parent continues to use negative messages and align with the child to try to undermine the parent, kids can begin to see that the targeted parent is not a bad person. This is the benefit of recognizing alienation and working with your kids to show them that you are still Dad or Mom and that you still love them with all your heart, no matter what the other parent is saying or doing. Be aware, however, that this recovery from the damage done by the alienator often takes years – if ever, in severe cases.

For many parents, negative brainwashing activities start immediately after the separation; so, parents should have current legal representation for the temporary and final orders regarding the children. In other cases, the actual alienating behavior doesn't begin until after the final orders have been signed.

In situations where you no longer have an attorney since the divorce is completed, it is essential to talk to a lawyer regarding your concerns as soon as you notice the issues developing. Talking to the other parent is the first step, especially if you have previously had at least a civil or calm relationship when working in the best interests of the child or children. Parents that are naïve alienators may be willing to listen to your concerns, especially if you speak to them without attacking or criticizing them.

It is essential to talk to an attorney for the other types of deeper alienation, including active and obsessive. Your lawyer will provide information on:

## Documentation

Document all examples of brainwashing or your ex's mental state. For your attorney to start helping you with your mental abuse case or having access or contact with the child or children, it will be important to start documenting. This can include several different issues such as canceled or no-showed visitations, changes in the duration of your time with the child or children, negative messages, or even negative statements that your ex-spouse makes about you in front of the children during the exchanges, or your child's outbursts at exchanges. Your attorney can provide outlines on how to document your ex's actions and your child's expressions showing emotional damage.

Some ways to document these outbursts by both your ex and your child:

- A smartphone's video camera
- iPhone users: your Voice Memos application
- Android users: your Voice Recorder application

If your lawyer doesn't object, start recording or audio taping disturbing events (your son leaving screaming voice mail messages, crying at visitation exchanges, etc.). It's one thing for you to talk under oath about how your child is mentally abused. It's another thing to let the judge hear it for him or herself.

Another element to document is all the troubles and incidences that happen from week to week. Why? Because one day, there's a good chance you'll need some reminders of your ex's actions. Also, it's helpful to fully document every ugly utterance, denied visitation, and outburst one day. Once your child is an adult, let them know that you documented every action because it concerned you so much. Then be prepared for your adult child to want to see it.

## Options

Many parents dread going back to court and facing the extreme costs of a prolonged custody dispute. Since this can run into the tens of thousands of dollars in legal fees, your attorney may be able to provide less costly options.

## Referrals

Attorneys especially established in any area, often have other professionals they work with to help reconciliation between parents and children of alienation. Don't hesitate to ask, as you may be surprised at the results of these referrals.

Avoid getting angry and upset at your child.

It is not uncommon for brainwashed children to only talk about the negative side of the targeted parent. They may make extremely hurtful comments to you as a parent, ones that you can't believe you're hearing. However, no matter how much it hurts to listen to put-downs or disrespectful remarks, do not take out your frustration on your children.

It is essential to remember that the other parent has entered into their campaign of negativity to block your child or children's love and affection for you. These kids will have lots of negative memories, images, and thoughts about you. This is particularly true if you have had several weeks, months, or years with minimal contact with the kids.

Often brainwashed children are extremely hostile towards the targeted parent. Their behaviors may include:

- Active disrespect: includes eye-rolling, swearing, and yelling. Indicating they "hate" the target parent and having no ability to see the effect of this hurtful language, nor showing any signs of remorse.
- Remaining extremely rigid in their inability to see anything positive or loving in your behavior.

- Talking about the alienating parent as the sole victim in the divorce.
- Interpreting past incidents inaccurately.
- Speaking negatively not just about you but even your entire family tree.
- Speaking in a disrespectful, indifferent way mirrors the alienating parent's tone (especially if the parent is narcissistic).

These statements and actions are hurtful, and the targeted parent has to learn to avoid taking these statements personally and acting out on them. It is entirely acceptable to let the child know that the comment hurts you and makes you very sad to hear that. But then follow up with a concise, unemotional statement that explains the truth. The key while doing this is not attacking or blaming your child or the alienating parent in any manner whatsoever.

An example:

Your son: "That's not fair... my Mom is right about you."

You: "I understand why you're upset. But such acting out against your sister won't be tolerated."

The "wrong" you: "Of course, there you go again siding with your Mom's hatred of me. It is fair, and I don't care what your Mom says about me."

## Text (SMS) Messages

Like email, text messages, or SMS messages are a great way to gently and positively tell your kids that you are thinking about them. The messages need to be relevant to the child, knowing you are interested and aware of their life. And they can be as simple as, "Just wanted to say I'm thinking about you :)."

Of course, texting "I love you" is a great way to let your child know you are thinking of them, but it can also be seen as routine if this is all that each text message is. You should also text questions about their upcoming game, something they are doing outside of school or anything else that they're up to.

Avoid sending too many text messages. However, otherwise, you risk making the children feel trapped between the brainwashing parent and yourself. A few text messages a week is a great balance; more is just needy or self-serving.

# WHEN YOUR EX INTERFERES WITH CONTACT AND COMMUNICATION

**E**veryone needs boundaries but narcissists more than most because they are essentially still children inside. Therefore, when communicating with them it is useful to think about how you would communicate with an infant rather than the adult they present as.

Be clear when and how communication can take place and enforce the consequences of not adhering to this. If you have agreed on calls with children that are in the other parent's care, set clear times when the children will be available and on what platform. This can be agreed on weekly, monthly, or annually depending on the lifestyle of the parents. Do not accept calls or texts outside of these times.

Equally, if you have calls agreed to the children when they are in their care, do not deviate from the times agreed. Even if they don't answer. A huge part of boundary setting is you maintaining them as well because the second you breach; the narcissist will see it as evidence that they can breach too. Yes, it will be hard but think about the bigger picture and the long-term peace you will get if you stick to it.

It is recommended to have one main platform for communication with the children with a backup platform just in case. So, Facetime is the preferred platform but if there is an issue with that, Skype. Nothing else unless agreed to by both parties.

The absolute best thing you can do here is to remain "no contact" and ride it out. Give them nothing. A strong sense of self is needed here and if this is something you struggle with; it is highly recommended to get professional help from an experienced therapist. When you step out of the abuser, victim, and enabler triangle, the narcissist has no choice but to find someone else to fill the spot you left open. They may use your children, so it is important to help build their resilience to withstand the pressure.

- Limit your contact with them as much as is humanly possible. If you have children use a mediator or communication app. This reinforces that their behavior is not acceptable, and they will get no attention from you when they "misbehave."

You will struggle to go no contact but there are ways for you to give yourself the space to heal whilst maintaining open communication about the children. Or the narcissist may be a family member who you aren't ready/willing to cut out of your life completely but recognize you need to limit your contact with them.

- Set up a clear strategy for dealing with "emergencies" including what constitutes an emergency

You know the narcissist will do anything and everything to trample all over your boundaries and using the children is easy pickings for them. They will go against your requests but use the "it's about the children" or "it's an emergency" to lure you into breaching your own boundaries. This just provides them with the confirmation that they are powerful and in charge.

# Emergencies

## Emergencies Could Include

- Health issues
- Unable to collect/return child(ren)
- Urgent appointment

Both of you need to agree to these but if they are unwilling, have them as your own standard.

Also clearly state what and how the other party will be notified about the emergency. Again, narcissists love to keep control so they will often keep you in the dark about situations or communicate through a channel never used so that they can say "I tried to notify you, it's not my fault you didn't check." Make sure it is something you can access but isn't intrusive. So, phone calls for example might be a definite "no" but a text is OK.

## Things to Consider in Case of an Emergency

Are they to be returned to the primary caregiver?

Does the parent they are with deal with the emergency and notify the other parent on an hourly basis?

Remember to consider your own personal boundaries whilst ensuring that the children's needs are met.

Also, be aware that going no-contact triggers a deep trauma within the narcissist and so this will be the most active and dangerous time. They will try:

- **Hoovering**—narcissists hate to lose supply and so they will attempt to lure you back in. It will start innocently enough with some form of contact. Maybe a "can I collect my stuff?" or "my friend told me you weren't at work, just wanted to check you are ok." It's bait to see if you are serious about no contact. If you are, you will probably skip ahead to smear campaigns. If not, love-bombing comes next.

- **Love-bombing**—they will lavish you with loving messages, gifts, promises of how they realize the error of their ways and you are the only person they love. It will be like music to your ears after the pain of separation and it will absolutely trigger your own abandonment wounds. But it is the same lies they told you in the relationship; no one can change in a few days or a week or even a month. Especially when it is a lifetime of behaviors. I know you want to believe them, but the reality is NPD requires years of specialized therapy to address the disorder. If they really have been through that the likelihood is that they won't contact you because they understand now how much they hurt you and would never want to re-open that wound for you. So, if they are back, they still lack empathy and simply do not care about the pain they caused.
- **Smear campaign**—you have resisted them so far and now they experience narcissistic injury. You have wronged them so badly that they have to punish you and they will use every means possible. Children, friends, family, professionals, pets... they will triangulate everyone into the drama and paint you as the abuser. In fact, they will use your firm "no contact" rule as "evidence" of how abusive you are being— "they won't even talk to me to tell me what happened." This is designed to weaken your resolve and make contact as well as giving them a clear narrative that they aren't the problem: you are. Nothing you do or say to any of the flying monkeys will change the story.

# YOUR CHILD REFUSES TO SEE YOU AT ALL

I t can be difficult for children to adjust when a parent has just left the family home. If your child refuses to see you or talk to you, you can do a few things.

First, do not get angry or upset. Your child may be punishing you for leaving them. They need to understand that you will be there for them, no matter what happens. Do not give up hope of being able to see your child again. It could take a long time — you may need patience and understanding and plenty of love, but eventually, your child will realize this is important for both of you.

If you are worried that your request will be refused, try not to show this. Children can be very wise, and they will soon work out that you are upset about the situation. You need to keep your emotions hidden until your child is ready to see you again.

If you feel it is necessary, try to talk to someone close to your child about their behavior.

- **Send cards or letters**—it may seem simple but telling your child that you love them and thinking of them often can go a long way in making someone feel wanted and cared for. Even if they don't write back, they might keep the card or letter as something of yours that they treasure and remember from their past.
- **Help support the children financially**—if you have left the family home with a child of your own, you may be able to ask a court for maintenance payments or arrears from your child's father. If your child is not living with their father, then there are no automatic rights to receive financial support, so you need to talk to a solicitor about whether this would be possible.
- **Consider mediation**—there is information on mediation for family disputes that might help you talk to your child and work out a way forward.
- **Keep yourself safe**—keep in mind the legal rules that protect you from harassment and abuse. You might want to get some advice if you feel threatened by your child.
- **Consider approaching the Child Maintenance Service (CMS)**—they may be able to help you with a maintenance application for your child.
- **Make an application for enforced contact**—if you have left the family home and have tried to communicate with your child by using the courts, local authority, or CMS that will order contact between your child and yourself.
- **Consider contacting a support group**—it may be that you are not alone, and other parents have left the family home and will be able to give you advice and support.
- **Consider whether it is necessary to make a criminal complaint against a parent**—if you have already left the family home and have had no contact with your child, you may want to speak to the police or social services about making a criminal complaint either assault or harassment.

- **Consider taking out an injunction against a parent**—if you are not comfortable with making an application at court, you may want to consider applying for an injunction against another parent.

# HOW TO PROTECT YOUR CHILD FROM ALIENATION AND LOYALTY CONFLICTS

Every parent worries about their child's future and whether they will find happiness in life. Some parents are also concerned about whether their children will withstand peer pressure or develop a sense of belonging around them. As you try to protect your children from the surrounding environment, you become worried about how much effort it takes to shelter them from social evils such as drugs, peer pressure, and abuse. Some parents find it difficult to understand that a child can have different values than their own. Some parents fear that their children might even be viewed unfavorably by their peers.

As a parent, you are willing to try and understand your child's values, but it will take a lot of effort. Some parents try to put their children in situations that they deem ideal for them, but this can cause other problems such as "enforced alienation."

Some parents believe that their children should be protected from opinions and situations that conflict with theirs. However, this can cause a child to feel alienated from society and lose their sense of belonging. As children try to form an identity for themselves, they will develop different opinions and feelings about the world around them. This is an important process for healthy development.

Loyalty conflicts occur when parents create extreme or strict rules, focusing on every aspect of their lives. Because the child has been exposed to this type of parenting from a very young age, they feel confused and unable to cope with other situations that involve peers.

Many parents try to shelter their children from abuse and bullying. Some focus on every little aspect of their lives, such as what they wear, who they talk to, and how long they spend on the computer. This kind of parenting can ruin a child's independence and self-esteem.

By avoiding these strategies, you can help your child develop independence and self-esteem by making them feel safe in the world around them. Children should be encouraged to spend time with their peers and become involved in activities that help them develop an identity for themselves.

When children feel alienated from the world, they can feel sad and withdrawn from society. These behaviors can cause them to lose the motivation to spend time with their peers and participate in social activities. If you are anxious that your child is feeling this way, you should seek mental health assistance immediately.

Parents should create a positive and healthy relationship with their children without trying to shelter them from the world. Children should be encouraged to develop an identity for themselves rather than conform to their parents' ideal image.

Children who are afraid of abuse or bullying should be encouraged to speak about their concerns. Parents should help their children discover ways of dealing with these situations immediately, rather than shelter them from these types of actions forever. Parents should try to understand that anything you do for their child is an investment in their future. No parent can guard their child against all peer pressures and social problems, but you will be doing your best to guide them into healthy choices when they face these types of situations as teenagers.

A loyal child can gain the trust of others; it means they are faithful to their parents or other close relatives. They can be loyal to friends and neighbors and loyal to a country, religion, or school. A child loyal to their parents and friends will make the right decisions later in life, have a positive attitude towards others, and have self-esteem.

A child loyal to their parents and friends uses good judgment and is committed. A child with good judgment knows what they should do in different situations; they can think clearly about different circumstances without letting their emotions get in the way.

# CAUSES OF LOYALTY CONFLICTS IN DIVORCED FAMILIES

Several children of divorced parents are forced to deal with loyalty conflicts. One parent plans to have the child's complete loyalty, while the other parent attempts to discredit this same child. The child's primary loyalty is towards the parent without custodial care, but the parent with custodial care wants to make it so that person feels isolated and alone. This is not only displayed in domestic situations but also in social circles such as sports teams and clubs.

Children of divorced parents attempt to find a balance between these two worldviews. They learn to see both sides, regardless of how difficult it is, and come up with solutions that make everyone happy. They try to understand each parent's motivations and feelings. For example, a child may be interested in the parent who has custody and demonstrates loyalty, but the other parent may feel threatened by this new interest. On the other hand, if they fail to show interest in the parent with custodial care, this parent may feel abandoned and isolated.

To resolve the problem, a child of divorced parents must balance these two conflicting interests. They must observe and understand each parent's emotional life while maintaining their loyalty to them both. This can be difficult for children who have been exposed to years of conflict among their parents. They do not know how to deal with family relationships without causing tension or upsetting their parents.

## Causes of Loyal Conflicts in Divorced Families

Loyal conflicts can be caused by any one or several of the following:

### Family Structure

Family structure is an essential aspect of loyal conflicts in divorced families. A typical structural pattern is the presence of an absent parent. One or both parents may choose to have little contact with or even be missing from the child's life; however, they maintain a close relationship with each other as an ex-spouse. The result is a long-standing issue in which one parent feels abandoned, and the other feels rejected.

A new dynamic is often created between a parent and their child following a divorce. This new dynamic is powerful to the child as they may feel obligated to act in a certain way because that is how they learned behavior from their parents. They may begin to emulate their parents' relationship, or they won't, but they will learn how to deal with divorce by observing their relationship with their parents.

One of the significant reasons divorce leaves an impression on children is that they feel deprived and rejected by one of the primary caretakers. This has been shown to lead to significant mental health problems.

Children of divorce need to make sense of what they have experienced. They need to know why it happened, what it means for them, and how they fit into the picture.

## Parental Conflict

Parental conflict is an essential aspect of loyal conflicts in divorced families. It can be seen that children are being denied some contact with one parent because of this conflict. This rejection is often a result of an ongoing parental feud that escalates into physical violence. Parental conflict can be divided into several categories, such as:

Children are often left confused and frustrated by these various types of conflict. They are also very aware that their parents are fighting, but they do not understand why. Parents may try to justify their behavior by saying it "isn't the child's business," but this only causes more confusion and frustration because they want to speak up but can't.

Children of divorced families are often left with a feeling of helplessness in this situation. They hear both sides arguing through walls and doors. They feel trapped in the middle of the conflict. Children are not the cause of conflict, but they often become the victims and are made to take sides.

## Social Stigma

One of the major causes of loyal conflicts in divorced families is social stigma. This is caused by "a social perspective emphasizing how people should behave in response to moral or legal standards." This includes, but is not limited to:

When a child becomes aware of this stigma, it often makes them feel that one parent is more important than the other. They are forced to decide whether they want to run and live with the parent who seems more socially acceptable or stay with the parent who appears less socially acceptable.

## Child's Behavior

Children of divorced families sometimes experience a change in behavior as a result of their parent's divorce. This can be attributed to the fact that they are attending two separate households. Therefore, their time is divided between the two households because they have to deal with their internal struggles.

The most important factor affecting children's behavior is the extent to which children feel isolated from one parent due to conflicting loyalty. Children feel isolated from one parent when they refuse to be loyal to them.

## Behavior of Parents

Parents are the role models for children. They educate their children on how to treat people and also how to behave in various situations. Therefore, if a child's parents are divorced, they may have trouble deciding who they should respect and admire more, as each parent is likely to have different principles upon which they govern their lives.

## Child's Relationships with Siblings and Peers

The relationship between siblings and peers can be affected by loyal conflicts as well. The struggle between being loyal to one parent or the other may make a child develop a hostile attitude towards their siblings. They may begin to see their siblings as enemies. Also, if their parents separate them, one sibling may be required to live with the parent, who is seen as less socially acceptable. This can be quite damaging for the sibling's relationships with the other children in that household.

## Family or Social Events

Another cause of loyal conflicts in divorced families is family and social events. A child may feel uncomfortable at family or public events as they may expect to see their parents in an argument or don't want to choose between them. They may refuse to participate in the event so that they do not have to make this decision.

# CONSEQUENCES OF LOYALTY CONFLICTS IN DIVORCED FAMILIES

Family relationships are the foundation for healthy functioning. When they are strained or severed, it has a trickle-down effect that can negatively impact all family members. Research has identified several consequences of divorce on children and adults.

The children of divorced couples have to deal with the harsh reality that their parents are not together. They often feel left out and misunderstood. They may have to deal with resentment on the part of one parent and hatred toward the other. Non-custodial parents often take a back seat to financial support from their ex-spouse. Helping children adjust to parental divorce and loss can be a taxing experience for them. Loyalty conflicts among parents can arise in divorced families because of issues ranging from finances, living arrangements, visitation rights, and child support to how work schedules will be handled.

Parental conflict can lead to behavioral problems in children. Children who witness or are exposed to parental conflict may turn to negative behaviors such as substance abuse, violence, or other unhealthy activities. They may express their feelings through aggression toward others, aggressive behavior at school, depression, and anxiety disorders.

Children whose parents are involved in bitter custody battles are more likely to have increased symptoms of depression and anxiety than those who live with non-custodial parents. The increased stress that both parents experience may increase the risk of depression for children residing with the custodial parent.

Children who live in homes with volatile family environments struggle with emotional, behavioral, and social problems. Their world is often cut off from other people or events because of the two opposing parents' competing claims on their time and attention. Children in these situations are more likely to have feelings of insecurity, anxiety, loneliness, and withdrawal. They start to believe that they cannot make their own decisions. They often have difficulty in school and may develop a victim mentality. Children who experience parental conflict are more likely to demonstrate behavior problems such as acting out, aggression, anxiety, depression, bedwetting, sleep problems, and poor peer relations than children who do not. They also tend to have a higher negative self-image and low self-esteem rates than those who live in non-conflictual households.

When parents cannot express feelings and emotions without arguing with one another, it can have a detrimental effect on the children. These children grow up with the impression that they are not as important as their parents, leading to low self-esteem and feelings of insecurity.

Children who have experienced parental divorce may be more likely to experience delayed onset of puberty because of the increased time they spend away from home while their parents are fighting over custody and visitation rights.

Adolescents and young adults struggle with peer rejection, ostracism, and even bullying due to the divorce. They believe that they have to choose their friends carefully or leave their school altogether.

Adults that have experienced divorce often struggle to bond with their children. Although bonds are made and strengthened over time, they are still affected by the end of the marriage. They may suffer from depression and anxiety or find it difficult to trust a potential romantic partner again after the divorce.

Some divorces are the result of domestic abuse. Although this is not common by any means, it does impact divorce when children are involved. Like all victims of domestic violence, children can suffer from psychological trauma that can last a long time after the abuser has left home.

Regardless of the severity of the conflict between their parents, children who live with both parents have a more secure relationship than they would if only one parent was still living in the home.

When there is a divorce, children may even be pressured by their friends and peers to go for the parent they want to live with. This can be problematic for many different reasons.

# HIGH CONFLICT CO-PARENTING SITUATION

C o-parenting with a high-conflict person is exhausting, and just keeping up with the documentation of all their bad behavior will seem like a second job some days. These apps take some of this burden off you and have protections to prevent some dirty tricks. You can even request that using one of the co-parenting apps is part of your parenting agreement.

## Important Components of the Plan

Your attorney or a quick Internet search should be able to provide you with the parenting plan guidelines for your state or local area. You will need to establish an agreement around the following items. Refer back for more information about custody and visitation. It should include:

- **Child support**—Which parent is the payor, the amount, and how it will be paid
- **Legal custody**—Who will be in charge of decision-making for the children
- **Physical custody**—Who is the residential parent
- **Parenting schedule**—Specifically when the children will be with each parent
- **Medical, dental, vision insurance, and expenses**—Which will cover the children, and how non-reimbursed expenses will be shared, reported and reimbursed
- **Other expenses**—Who will pay what, and how reimbursement or expense sharing will occur.

When dealing with a high-conflict person, a verbal agreement is never sufficient. If you have young children, think ahead, and include all expenses that you believe might come up for your child, such as:

- Clothing
- Daycare
- School tuition, uniforms, and supplies
- School lunches
- Extracurricular activities, fees, and equipment/supplies
- Auto insurance, fuel, and maintenance
- Haircuts and personal expenses
- Cell phone
- Prom, homecoming, and other special-occasion clothes and expenses
- College entrance exams
- College visits
- College tuition, books, and expenses

It's important to detail how the expense is to be shared and how the parties will notify each other of the expense, how payment will be made, and within what time frame the payment should be made—the more specific, the better. Leaving things too general opens the door for the high-conflict person to find a loophole and will leave you frustrated. Without a legal agreement in place, it will be difficult to get a high-conflict person to negotiate or even agree on anything.

## Set a Firm Schedule

Make sure that you promote a relationship between the children and their other parent. Suggest a schedule that you believe is reasonable, and then stick to it.

If you or your spouse work unusual schedules (police, firefighter, shift work), then suggest a time split based on the number of hours per month and schedule that month (or every two weeks) as soon as the work schedule comes out for the next period. If that person fails to communicate their work schedule within X days to coordinate a parenting schedule, they will forfeit their parenting time for that period.

Be specific. That is critical with high-conflict people. Allow no wiggle room because they will keep pushing.

## Communicate in Writing

If you aren't able to use a co-parenting app, e-mail is your next best option. Phone calls with a high-conflict person can easily get out of hand, and you'll have no documentation as to your agreement. You must be able to show written proof that your partner agreed to the visitation schedule or the expense sharing that they are now not complying with. See Sharing Information for ideas to communicate about the children.

## Document

Document the efforts you have made to come to an agreement and to follow the temporary court orders. Also, document any behavior by your spouse that is uncooperative or not in the children's best interest. Make notes if your partner picked the children up or dropped them off late, if they took them out of state without approval, or failed to pay expenses. Write down any nasty comments your partner makes in front of the children or anything your children relay that they experienced at their other parent's house.

## You Can Say No

You don't have to agree to schedule changes or other variations to an agreed-upon parenting plan. Yes, you should demonstrate that you are cooperating, but continued requests for changes, particularly last-minute ones, do not need to be agreed to. You won't decrease their anger or high-conflict behavior by being accommodating. You'll set a precedent that they can continue to do whatever they please without regard to the agreement.

## Don't Take the Bait

Your spouse will try everything to get you to react, back down, or give up. You deserve a fair settlement, and your children deserve to have you in their lives. Keep your cool, speak assertively, and respond. The way to win with a high-conflict person is to manage your emotions and not give them any fuel for their arguments.

## Kids First

Every action and decision in divorce should be made with the best interest of the children in mind. That includes your language, behavior, parenting, and cooperation with your co-parent. Unless proven otherwise, the court will work under the assumption that civil co-parenting and equal time with each parent is best for the child. They assume that because it's usually true.

Regardless of how your spouse is behaving, it's still critically important to take the high road for your children and advocate for yourself in divorce.

# How to Resolve Common Issues in Co-Parenting

Co-parenting with a high-conflict person is bound to be filled with struggles. My advice to you is this: Your high-conflict partner will not follow the rules of decency when it comes to co-parenting. Decide right now that you will stop fighting to change things you cannot change.

You have the ability to either take the conflict up a notch or dial it back. Escalating the conflict isn't good for you or your kids. If your spouse always sends the clothes back dirty even though you asked them to send them back clean, let it go. Choose your battles. Only fight the ones that matter.

What are the issues that matter, and how can you attempt to resolve them?

## Schedule Changes

You must be flexible with them so they will be flexible with you. What if you get the chance to go on a great boating trip and want to swap weekends? Shouldn't you extend the same courtesy? Ideally, yes.

Assume best intentions and accommodate their request. Then ask them for a parenting time change and see how they respond. If you're not getting what you're giving, then the schedule stays the schedule. Period. It's harder on you with no flexibility, but it's one less battle you have to fight with them.

## Expenses

If you've gotten temporary orders or made an agreement, the types of expenses and how they will be paid should be clear. Otherwise, the best practice would be to scan the receipt and attach it to an e-mail explaining the expense, the other parent's share, and when/how you are requesting payment. Typically, 14 to 30 days is reasonable for reimbursement. If you don't receive payment by the date requested, send a brief e-mail reminder asking for payment. If they owe you more than one outstanding receipt, continue to send monthly statements listing each item and the total amount owed.

If you have court orders outlining your partner's responsibility, you may be able to show them to a school, doctor, or sports team, so you are only financially responsible for your share. Some will honor this arrangement and hold the other parent accountable for the remainder of the balance.

It is, unfortunately, common for high-conflict people to be financially abusive. They don't care that it hurts their children. If the behavior continues and what they owe becomes excessive, you may need to ask the court for relief.

## Information Sharing

The other parent should be sharing information with you just as you are sharing it with them. If that isn't happening, arrange to add yourself to the school or activity e-mail or notification system. Call and explain your situation.

## Involving the Children

You know it's best not to bad-mouth your spouse or put the children in the middle, but that may not stop your partner from doing it. They may tell the children untrue things, use the children as spies or messengers, or say things about you in front of them.

# Exceptions to Co-Parenting

If your partner has been abusive, has an addiction or mental illness, or otherwise puts the children's safety at risk, act surely and quickly. Talk to your attorney and look for steps you need to take. Request sole custody and a protection order. Ask for supervised visitation only. Request these at least temporarily until the court has a chance to investigate. Prepare your documents and be ready to prove your case. "He said/she said" may not be enough to win the day.

Ask that guardian ad litem be appointed. This is an attorney who will act as a neutral third party on behalf of your child and may testify as an expert witness.

Without the court's backing, it's dangerous to prevent your spouse from seeing the children even if you have concerns. The court may view this as uncooperative or adversarial on your part.

# PREPARATION FOR A CUSTODY EVALUATION

I f you seek permanent custody of your children, your case will be stronger if you have custody when you file for divorce. The laws of most states say that whoever has custody when the divorce papers are filed, keeps custody until the court orders something different. This is to avoid parents stealing the children back and forth from each other.

There are two kinds of custody in most states, often called Physical Custody and Legal Custody. Physical custody is where the children are, which parent they live with most of the time. Legal custody involves the right to make or participate in decisions such as medical care for the child or which school a child will attend. Most states also have the concept of Joint Custody, in which each parent exercises some custody rights over the child after the divorce. The alternative to Joint Custody may be called Separate Custody. There are different kinds of custody in more detail because they usually come into play when the court enters the final custody order. Speak about "custody," unless the context indicates otherwise, I'm talking about Physical Custody—which parent the child is living with, where the child's principal residence is.

In contentious situations, to make sure there is no question of who has custody at the time of filing, I've had my client take the children and a friend with him to the courthouse. The friend sits with the kids in the car outside the courthouse while my client goes inside to file the divorce papers I prepared. However, if you plan to ask for custody, don't allow your wife to take care of the kids for six months of separation, then snatch the kids the day before you file.

One final warning: While it is best to have custody when you file, if you effectively try to kidnap the children or do anything that will seriously upset them to gain early custody, that will come back to bite you later. Talk to your attorney before you plan anything tricky.

You should not do the following unless your attorney approves before you take any of these steps:

- Move the children out of a school they have been attending.
- Start the children with a new daycare provider.
- Take or send the children across a state line.

Divorce is very upsetting for children. For the children's benefit and to demonstrate that you are a careful parent, pay close attention to their emotional reactions. Phone their teachers and daycare providers and tell them about the family situation, so these people are in a better place to assist your child.

If you have the guidance of your children and have any reason to believe your spouse might try to snatch them, school and daycare are some of the most common locations for a snatch. You need to notify the school principal, your children's teachers, and the daycare provider about the situation and make certain who is to pick up the children. Deliver a letter stating you are in a divorce proceeding and instructing the school or daycare center to release your child only to you or someone you designate in writing. If the events leading up to the divorce have been nasty and that nastiness has affected any of your children, you should consider professional counseling for them. Your attorney can recommend possible counselors.

Quite frankly, some of the counseling is for the benefit of the children, but some are also to inoculate yourself against accusations that you're a careless parent.

If the laws of your state are that whichever parent has custody when the divorce papers are filed keeps custody until trial, and you have such custody, you're not going to be asking the judge to change that. But, if your spouse has custody and that's not what you want, your attorney will need to file a Motion for Temporary Custody.

The Motion for Temporary Custody will state why custody should be changed, so this is often the start of mud thrown in the divorce trial.

After a motion is filed, it will be set for a hearing. A temporary custody hearing is no different than a permanent custody hearing. Each side presents evidence relevant to what custody arrangements are in the children's best interests, and the judge makes a decision. However, after a temporary custody hearing, the judge's custody order is temporary and continues only until the judge enters a permanent order at the end of the case.

Usually, an attorney will want to file a motion for temporary custody quickly. Suppose the children have been living with one parent for three months after the separation. In that case, the parent with temporary custody has a powerful argument that switching temporary custody will upset the children after so long. If the final custody order switches them back, this will cause unnecessary emotional burdens.

Many judges are not excited about hearing custody testimony twice for temporary custody and a second time for permanent custody. (They like the idea of multiple temporary custody hearings even less.) Sometimes, a judge will respond to a motion for temporary custody by moving the entire divorce proceeding to an earlier date on her trial docket so that permanent custody can be determined. Sometimes, a judge will respond to a motion for temporary custody by ignoring it or setting and postponing a hearing several times.

If the judge sets a temporary custody hearing quickly, it's not easy to organize compelling evidence within a few days. If you're asking for temporary custody, you should have a good chance of winning because losing a temporary custody hearing may put you in a disadvantageous position in a later permanent custody trial.

On the other hand, a quick temporary custody hearing is just as hard for the other side to deal with. If you have some smoking-gun evidence—a cell phone video of your wife in bed with her lover with your five-year-old daughter lying between them, for example, or testimony from your wife's landlord that he is evicting her because the kitchen is full of rotting garbage—you stand a better chance of ambushing your wife's lawyer at a temporary custody hearing when he is unprepared to respond to such evidence. He has had much less time to discuss damaging evidence with his client than he will have before a trial in permanent custody.

Sometimes, a Motion for Temporary Custody provides a basis for negotiation between attorneys for the parties. A hearing is going to cost both parties some significant attorney's fees and make the entire divorce more expensive. Maybe the custodial parent is discovering he doesn't like being the sole caretaker of the children as much as he thought he would. Perhaps the parties can agree on a temporary custody arrangement that puts the spouse who started without custody of the children in a better position to ask for permanent custody later. Maybe the wife will give up custody of the children if the husband agrees to pay credit card bills.

As a general proposition, more Motions for Temporary Custody are settled by negotiation than by trial, but you can't be sure that will be the outcome in your case. You can see why beginning your divorce with custody can be so important. While each parent has an equal right to custody under the law, if the children have been living with a parent for one year and nothing terrible has happened to them, it's hard for the non-custodial parent to make a case that leaving the children in that situation permanently is a bad idea. It's also easy for the custodial parent to argue that the children have already gone through enough trauma without adding another move and, perhaps, different schools or daycare providers and different friends in a new neighborhood to that mix.

If you want permanent custody of your children, starting your case with custody is important enough to defer the formal filing of papers until you have custody. Usually, it's safer if you file first than waiting for your spouse to file. Your spouse can drive to the courthouse with the kids in the car just as easily as you can.

Suppose you anticipate a disagreement with your spouse about custody. In that case, your best bet is to keep quiet about any divorcing ideas and hire a good lawyer to help you plan a strategy that will strengthen your chances of a good custody outcome.

# THE CHILD AND THE CUSTODIAL PARENT: POSITIVE AND NEGATIVE ASPECTS

A custodial parent is a parent who has lost their custody rights over their child by going into an agreement to work in exchange for having the child live with them. A non-custodial parent is usually a mother but can also be one of the two male parents in a blended family.

Generally, people in a blended family favor a shared custody arrangement and are unhappy when the other parent wants to end the agreement or deny any visits.

Custody is defined as having legal rights and responsibilities over a minor child. It is often very emotionally charged and controversial. Many cases go through the courts over custody disputes of children. When parents separate, they usually have joint custody arrangements, which means both parents are equally involved in their child's life.

The relationship between a child and the custodial parent cannot be perfect. In other words, there are both positive and negative aspects to being in the custody of one parent compared to two. These differences may arise for many reasons, but they may also stem from the fact that the laws concerning custody, in general, are more lenient on mothers than on fathers.

After all, it seems logical to award custody to the one parent who demonstrates a greater ability to provide care through employment or income, is more stable, and takes care of the children.

In other words, mothers have a distinct advantage in determining the custody arrangements in family cases. This is a product of the fact that children are more likely to be dependent on their mothers than the father, whether it is due to age, work, etc.

## Positive Aspects

- The child has one home and one family identity.
- The custodial parent can spend more time with the child.
- There is reduced financial strain on the custodial parent.
- There is a reduced risk of conflict between divorced parents about dividing their assets because all assets are in only one name (the custodial parent's name).

The child may be less confused about why one parent is absent or missing in their life and how they feel when they are away.

The child may be more satisfied with their role relationship with the custodial parent than the rest of their family, despite their closeness to other family members.

Parents who have been rendered a single custodian of their children typically feel closer since they are now forced to rely on each other for all parenting responsibilities and decisions regarding children's arrangements.

No custody orders are completely negative. There are, however, many more negative aspects to it than there are to joint custody arrangements. Custodial parents tend to be isolated in their homes and become quite lonely since they have no outside social contacts, especially when they have very young children. They may even feel imprisoned or trapped by the child's behavior because their power as a parent is severely limited by decisions made by childcare agencies, such as those concerning schooling and medical care for the child.

## Negative Aspects

- The child may have trouble adjusting to a new family situation.
- The child may function better with two parents.
- There is an emotional strain on the custodial parent to balance a new relationship with the child with one with the other parent.
- If there are two divorces, both parents will be asked about the assets and debts of each, which can be very harmful to both parents.

Custodial parents can be overbearing to control their children, especially as they get older. The child may no longer listen to the parent because they think of themselves as an adult and not a child. It is possible that the child will rebel against authority after being raised by one parent and following only their rules. This can create a tense relationship between parent and child.

There are also many cases where custody of a child is given to a parent who is not fit for the task. The parent that has been given custody may be unfit mentally, emotionally, or physically to take care of a child. In many situations, this can lead to neglect and abuse or the inability of the custodial parent to properly provide for the child, especially if they do not have jobs or stable lifestyles.

Psychological problems in children can also stem from being raised by one parent. This is the case if the mother believes the father to be a threat to her or the child or has feelings of insecurity towards him. In these cases, the child will likely grow up believing their parent's fears about their father.

Children raised by only one parent often have low self-esteem or feel that they cannot live up to the standards of one parent if they are unable to do so for both parents. The child's feelings of disappointment grow as they realize that there is not a second parent to lean on when life gets complicated.

Children who are sent to live with extended family for the period that their parent's divorce usually stay with the mother's side of the family. They will feel that they do not belong in their father's family, or they may feel scared about staying in a different home than where they were accustomed to.

Custody disputes are frequent and can be quite emotional. Children may not acknowledge why they have to move or why their family is split up. This can cause insecurity in the child and make them feel that they are losing their childhood.

If the child moved multiple times while growing up, this could be an even bigger source of insecurity; this is more common than one would think.

When both parents are involved in raising a child, they have been exposed to the same influences; therefore, this helps them learn about each other's beliefs and values.

# HOW TO DEAL WITH PARENTAL ALIENATION

## Contact Is Important

I t is crucial for you, as an alienated parent, to show your kids, you're there for them. Don't wait and let them come to you. Keep trying to contact them.

It may mean to text your kids if they have a phone or send emails. It may mean that you turn up at arranged pickups, regardless of whether or not your ex intends to let the kids go to your contact.

Don't wait for your kids to contact you. You need to be the one who is reaching out and making an effort. They need to feel that you haven't given up and that you're still trying to be there for them.

When you do speak to them, don't mention the other parent negatively. This isn't about getting your kids to understand your side or turning them back to you by pointing out what their other parent has done wrong.

## Positivity

Always be positive about the other parent. You can think that your ex is the living embodiment of Satan himself, you can even say it out loud, but you really shouldn't say it in front of your kids.

Even in the most amicable of separations, children can feel that they're caught in the middle. With an alienating parent, this is escalated to extremes. However, you should always try to be positive about your children's other parent in front of your children. Your family and friends will want to help, so talk to them about your frustrations, but never do it in front of your children.

If you can't be entirely positive about your ex, and as long as it's age-appropriate, you could say something like 'I'm sorry you had to hear negative things about me,' or 'I'm sorry that you're caught in the middle of this adult stuff, but you should know that both of your parents love you.'

## Letters, Emails, and Gifts

While almost all of our lives seem digital, kids will get a kick out of receiving something in the mail. So, send cards, letters, and small gifts.

Keep your letters positive and happy. Don't say that you miss them or that you can't wait to see them. Instead, tell them that you love them, and you're excited they're having a good time with your ex.

Many alienated parents don't do this because they fear that their ex will intercept anything sent in the mail. If this is the case, send everything by recorded delivery. You can say to your ex that you had sent something, and could see it was delivered, so you want to check if your children got it or enjoyed it. This may be enough for your ex to give your letters to the kids. If not, give all the evidence of delivery to your legal representative, and let them deal with it in court.

Whichever route works for you, be aware that this is not the time to go off on a tangent about your ex in general. The issue is around your children receiving mail, so make sure you stick to that issue.

## Be Interested in Their Interests

You can ask them about any extracurricular activities, friends, or even just how their day was at school. However, some alienated children don't react well to even the most innocent of questions and can become shut down, avoidant, or even hostile.

If that describes your children, there are still ways you can show them you're interested. If you have friends who have children a similar age, ask what their kids are into. You could pick up magazines, browse websites, and look at the trends for video games, TV shows, movies, music, and apps.

## Be Involved at School

Alienating parents don't often share important information about the school, events, sports games, or anything else going on in your child's life. One way you can circumvent this is to talk to the school directly and ask them to keep you updated.

When you have the information, attend the events. If the alienating parent has told the kids that you don't care but still come to their events, they will start to question the idea that you don't care. They will start to realize that you do care as you keep coming to support them.

Many alienated parents don't go to events because they don't want to have any confrontation with the alienating parent or embarrass their child by causing a scene. You can still attend without it needing to be a drama. You should speak to your legal representative about the best way to do this.

For some, these issues can be worked out in mediation. For others, it can be agreed in court that both parents attend and sit at opposite ends of the hall, field, or wherever the event is. Some may need to arrange a schedule for one parent to attend on one date and the other parent to attend another.

# Technology

Depending on the ages of your kids, technology can be your best friend. Social media, email, and messaging apps can all help you keep in touch with your kids.

You could use an app to create a photo album and keep adding photos and videos to it. Add family photos, but also, you could add photos or videos that your kids would find interesting. You can keep the album private so that only you and your kids have access.

## Video Games

You also shouldn't discount video games. If you're a gamer, many games allow online co-op play, so you can play and talk to your kids.

Kids like playing video games because they're fun, they're challenging, and they can be creative in them. They can also get a sense of achievement from a video game, such as when they beat a particularly difficult level or build an amazing building.

If you're involved, either in person or online, they will remember how they beat the level and that you were there to help. This also helps create a disconnect in their minds between their memories and feelings of you and your ex's feelings about you.

## Text

If your kids have their phones, then text them. Don't text too often but send messages to let them know that you were thinking about them and love them.

Don't send the same message all the time either, as they can begin to think that it's a routine for you, and you don't mean it. Ask about school or an activity they enjoy or share something you've seen and thought they would like or news about their favorite band.

You should still text a few times a week, even if your child doesn't reply.

## The Extended Family

You need to keep your extended family involved in your children's lives. It will help your children realize that they have a wider family than just your ex and their family members. It will show your kids that not everyone shares your ex's opinion when they hear your family members speaking positively about you.

However, before you throw your kids in at the deep end, it might be a good idea to talk with your family and set out some ground rules.

The first thing you need to be certain of is that nobody will say anything negative about your ex. They're allowed to think that your ex is the devil, but they absolutely cannot say it in front or on earshot of the kids. Make sure everyone knows that those conversations are only to be had when the kids aren't there.

Make sure that your family knows that if they have to talk about the other parent, they do so respectfully and without hostility. Remind them to call your ex by their title — use 'mum' or 'dad.' They'll need to avoid calling your ex by their name.

You also need to be clear that your family shouldn't ask the kids questions about your ex or anything that happens at that house. There's no way to ask these questions without it looking like your family is snooping, which will not go down well with your kids. Spending time with you and your family must be positive and completely free from any 'them vs. us' mentality.

## Don't React to Hurtful Comments

Kids can be very matter of fact, and they might not notice that the things they say are hurtful. They won't understand that saying something like 'mummy says I can't love you' causes painful emotions.

It's extremely important that you don't react in a way that shows you feel angry or upset. Instead, remain calm and explain that, of course, your child can love both parents.

## Hostile Children

Some children are so alienated that they have many negative memories of you. These memories can be entirely false and planted by the alienating parent, but your child has been taught that they are true.

Extremely hostile children can be very disrespectful and can be entirely unable to see anything positive about you or their time with you. They can tell you they hate you or speak to you in the same way as the alienating parent does. They can idolize the alienating parent and believe that this parent can do no wrong. They can make similar comments about your extended family.

These children don't show any remorse for what they're saying or see that it hurts them. It's incredibly important to stay calm; however, you should tell them that what they've said has been hurtful. After following up with a short factual statement — for example, 'it hurts me that you feel that way, but I love you and only want what's best for you,' or 'I understand you feel angry, but you still need to be nice to your cousins.'

Never say negative about the alienating parent. Telling your child that the alienating parent is lying will only serve to further alienate your child.

# DEALING WITH FALSE ALLEGATIONS OF CHILD ABUSE AND DOMESTIC VIOLENCE

A s a parent, you know that allegations of abuse are taken very seriously by Child Protective Services. These false allegations can have major implications on your child, family, and personal life. You might end up in court with no safety net fighting for custody of your children and a restraining order against you, which can impact your professional relationships as well as personal associations.

In circumstances where you are in a family dispute, and the court is taking allegations of child or spousal abuse seriously as a parent, you should prevent your children from being taken away from you. Be prepared and in a position where you can defend yourself against false allegations and be able to win the case in court if all else fails.

## Step 1: Demote the False Allegations

You can question the credibility of your accuser. In most cases, the person making the accusations seeks financial gain or revenge and will not be truthful in their accusations. For example, how long have they known you, their true intentions, and what do they stand to gain if these allegations go through.

## Step 2: Monitor Your Alleged Victim

You should also be aware of the character of the person who is making false allegations against you. If it is someone who has a history of telling lies often, that can be used to dispute their credibility. You can hire private investigators to get information about them and present that in court as evidence.

If you observe people who are supporting your accuser, be wary of them. They are likely to be the ones who have given false testimony against you.

# Step 3: Consult with your Lawyer

It is important to consult with your lawyer in steps 1 and 2 as they can help you strategize on winning the case and not fighting it just for the sake of fooling people into thinking that everything is fine. They will know what steps to take and how to make a strong case in court.

# Step 4: Document Everything

Your lawyer will know that the most important thing is to document everything and anticipate the kind of questions you may be asked in court so they can get the answers for you. Listen carefully to your lawyer and follow their instructions.

If there is something you do not understand, ask them to explain it to you so that it will benefit your case. You will be better at defending yourself and winning back custody of your children when you know more.

# Step 5: Don't Make a Statement or Answer Questions without your Lawyer

Never make a statement in the case without consulting with your lawyer first. If you are asked to answer questions outside of when you and your lawyer are present, refuse to answer them as it can hurt your case later. The only one who can help you in this situation is an experienced attorney familiar with these types of cases.

# Step 7: It is possible to Win a Case

If you have been able to prepare yourself in the first few hours or days after it happened, you can win a case with allegations of abuse. So, if you are not guilty and have taken the proper steps to defend yourself, you can win.

# Step 8: Seek Counseling for your children

False allegations are very traumatizing for your children as they suffer the negative impacts when they are removed from their families. Do everything to get them the help they need to cope with or recover from the trauma of being separated from you.

# Step 9: Seek Counseling for Yourself

Do not be surprised if you are traumatized by what is happening and have difficulty coping with everything. Suppose you think you cannot manage this and your children, seek counseling for yourself so that you can get better and fight back.

Sometimes false allegations can be made against you or your child, in which the person who is accusing you is the one who is guilty of abuse. You will need to have a solid case that will show that they are not credible, and this needs to be supported by evidence and witnesses.

You should think about hiring a private investigator to watch the person making the allegations. You can also get them to expose their private life on social media, such as social media websites so that it will be easier for you to assemble evidence against them. You should also present this information in court so that the judge and lawyer know that they are not credible and there is no real evidence against you or your child.

# TIPS FOR DEALING WITH YOUR ABUSIVE EX IN A CUSTODY HEARING

We know that just the mention of your abusive ex can set off a stress mechanism in your brain that leads to some serious anxiety. You may also worry about what will happen at the custody hearing and how you'll react when seeing them. There are some tips on how to cope with this challenge and strategies for dealing with your abusive ex at a custody hearing.

When you first had the child in your safe and protective care, you likely felt an immense amount of stress as they were also under incredible levels of stress. You may have already developed coping mechanisms which are working well for you. The anxiety surrounding the custody hearing is typically not similar to the stress from early on in your relationship while fighting for custody. Rather than feeling anxious about future events, you might be experiencing anxiety symptoms as a result of deep-seated insecurities stemming from the abuse you suffered while in your abusive relationship. To prepare for the custody hearing, you need to know what you will say and do when in court. This is best done in advance, giving you time to prepare yourself, so prepare ahead by doing some practice runs. Get some information from someone who knows a lot about this process who can help you understand what will happen. It could be a family member or your lawyer. Here are some other tips that can help you when you get to court:

## Be Informed

You need to know all the facts of the case from both sides. Considering how volatile and emotional this process can be, it is best to get as much information as possible in advance so you'll be prepared for what will happen. Your lawyer can give you some tips on what a judge will be looking for and how they may question the parties. You can also read the materials that were prepared for both sides if they are available.

## Stay Calm

It is easy to get emotional and, when you do, you'll likely have problems doing what you need to do in court; so, it's important to keep your cool and stay focused the whole time. A patient approach will help you get through this process without any serious stress or anxiety.

## Don't Be Afraid of Your Ex

They may bully you a bit, but you need to keep in mind that they are not in the right mind and are probably trying to manipulate you into doing things they want. Remember that underneath all their anger, abuse, and aggression is someone who cares about you very much.

## Be Prepared to Be a Witness at the Custody Hearing

The court will likely ask your ex some questions, so it's important to be prepared for these kinds of situations. It will also help if you have a list of questions you want to ask your ex or their lawyer. Keep in mind that being in the position of questioning your ex's character may not be the best tactic to use. This isn't the time to get into a battle for who is right or wrong, but rather focus on what is best for your child.

## Don't Try to Be Perfect; Just Be Yourself

You will likely do better and find it easier to concentrate when you're more relaxed. You need to do some things when you're in court but try not to overdo it and let the stress get to you.

## Don't Be Terrified to Use Your Lawyer as a Consultant

During the decision-making process, you may have problems deciding what actions to take. You can ask your lawyer for help with this, and they will give you good advice about how you should proceed.

Now that you understand some tips on how to deal with your abusive ex at a custody hearing, it's time to get prepared for this challenging process. Putting together a strategy in advance will give you the best chance of moving forward without fear.

# PREPARING FOR TRIAL, TESTIFYING, AND DEALING WITH THE TYPES OF QUESTIONS ATTORNEYS ASK DURING CROSS-EXAMINATION IN THE UNITED STATES

**M**any people have a hard time preparing for trial. The thought of taking the stand and being questioned by an opposing attorney can be disturbing and intimidating to many people. Jurors have similar feelings as witnesses and often feel overwhelmed during trial preparation. You must know what to expect when you come face-to-face with your opponent in Court. Narcissists are very controlling and manipulative, and they want to win. They are good at spinning lies and making other people look bad. It is important to have a plan and stick to your guns. Narcissists are very persuasive and can play the "victim" very well. It is for this reason that you mustn't take their comments personally.

The narcissist wants to win and will use any sneaky means to do it. Remember, they are pathological liars and can stage Oscar-winning performances in courtrooms. Pathological narcissists are the most poisonous and dangerous opponents that can be faced in any court.

The types of cases in which you may be involved are the following:

- Criminal proceedings in which you have fallen victim to a crime committed by a pathological narcissist.
- Divorce proceedings, in which goods/money are at stake.
- Child custody cases.
- Return procedure for goods/money due.

If it is a divorce case, the narcissist will appear confident and calm. At the same time, the subjugated former partner will have already been severely trampled by this ruthless individual in the months and years preceding the trial and will often appear stressed and lacking self-confidence and the law.

If you are in this situation, not having conversations and avoiding eye contact with the narcissist inside or outside the courtroom will be essential for you. Better to find a place on the sidelines where to sit outside the courthouse while waiting or at intervals so that the narcissist and his lawyers and followers cannot intimidate you or make you nervous.

Many people who face a narcissist in court fear that he will be able to manipulate there too and that the lies told are believed. It is essential to ensure that the legal representative of your choice is aware of what Narcissist Personality Disorder is. A lawyer who knows nothing is likely to be manipulated by the narcissist and can advise you to negotiate when it is not in your best interest to do so.

If the narcissist pushed you to the limit in the past, now it's up to your lawyers to play hard.

Narcissists are likely to react when their lives are exposed, and their bad behaviors brought to light. Eventually, you reveal information that they had no intention of letting the world know, so their anger can become uncontrollable. Often their lawyers do everything to keep them "good," calm, and content (a rather tricky, if not impossible task).

They probably have hidden or diverted goods: they are very skilled in concealing their earnings.

Is it possible to empower a narcissist in Court? Of course, but one must be well prepared. It is essential to be armed with irrefutable, undeniable, and corroborated evidence.

Avoid giving the narcissist credible alternative scenarios to the facts. A skilled lawyer knows how to put a narcissist in trouble with the right questions, to remove the wind from the sails subtly but effectively.

Example:

- I am led to believe that you are entirely qualified in your profession. Excuse me, what is your highest academic qualification? So, it doesn't have a formal qualification, I understand. "
- Contradicting or diminishing the narcissist's inflated vision of himself and his fragile self-esteem will shatter.
- A trained lawyer knows how to play with words so that a narcissist understands that he has no control over everything and everyone.
- When we are in the confines of the courtrooms, we must stay as far away from the narcissist as possible and never look in his direction. The fact that never being looked at causes a narcissistic wound: they hate being ignored!
- As we know, the narcissist believes he is above the law and not subject to the limitations of ordinary citizens. As for them, they are superior to anyone in the courtroom, including the judge and lawyers. Nobody can have the audacity to make them responsible for their actions! Anyone who testifies against them will be labeled a liar and corrupt.
- Avoid showing any reaction to their words or behavior. They knew how to step on your Achilles heels first, and they will try again. Make sure these attempts are accepted with indifference.
- It can be challenging to communicate to magistrates and lawyers how unacceptable the behavior of a pathological narcissist has been.

- The goal of a good lawyer will be to snatch any information from the Court and lead them to discredit themselves when their explosive fury makes its appearance.
- Always remember to tell the truth. Never be tempted to beautify the truth or paint a fake picture.

And remember never to drop to the narcissist level.

# CONCLUSION

I t is unfortunate that many people in this world are narcissists. Narcissism is a debilitating condition that can cause severe pain to the narcissist and those around them. When it comes to co-parenting with a narcissistic ex, both parties must make choices that will allow for an environment where their child can thrive.

For this to occur, the non-narcissist must make certain sacrifices, and the narcissist must repair their damaged self-esteem. While this process is an ongoing one, the narcissist must choose to do what it takes to repair their relationship with others and themselves.

It is important to note that you cannot control another person. It is your job to take care of yourself. You cannot change the actions of another person. You can choose, however, how you will react to those actions. It's essential to remember that you played no part in forming the narcissist's disorder, nor can you cure it. Abuse is not about power and control; it's about pain and disempowerment. A narcissist may use emotional and physical abuse to feel powerful and in control when they feel powerless.

As difficult as it may be, you must set healthy boundaries. This is your life, and you should be treated with the same dignity and respect that anyone else would expect. You are not your children's property or the property of your narcissistic ex. You must make choices that will allow for a healthy environment for everyone involved. It is also important to realize that narcissistic behavior will always be a part of the relationship you have with your ex. There are years of pain and dysfunction that your ex must deal with to become well again.

Remember, you must take care of yourself as well as your child. You must protect both parties from the emotional chaos that may be occurring. It is recommended to seek therapy for yourself to heal from this difficult situation and make decisions based on what's best for yourself and your child.

The goal is to form an environment where the narcissistic ex can learn how to treat others to respect and honor them.

You must also protect your child from the negative effects of co-parenting with an ex who has such a severe disorder. It will be essential for you to teach him what it means to have boundaries and what it means to respect themselves. This may take some time, but in the end, you will both be glad you did.

Keep in mind that the non-narcissist is not responsible for the narcissist. You are the victim of abuse and must make choices that best suit you, your child, and your family unit. The narcissist's actions have nothing to do with you; they are merely symptoms of an underlying problem.

I hope you have found these statements to help you come to terms with your situation. It is my sincere goal for you to also gain insight into some of the behaviors that may be occurring in your relationship. And when you feel like there is no way out, remember this: You are a worthy individual and deserve a deep sense of self-respect, happiness, and love.

CPSIA information can be obtained
at www.ICGtesting.com
Printed in the USA
LVHW060256080622
720776LV00011B/402